Transformative Quality

The Emerging Revolution in Health Care Performance

Transformative Quality

The Emerging Revolution in Health Care Performance

Mark Hagland

Foreword by Jeffrey C. Bauer, PhD

CRC Press
Taylor & Francis Group

A PRODUCTIVITY PRESS BOOK

Productivity Press
Taylor & Francis Group
270 Madison Avenue
New York, NY 10016

Library of Congress Cataloging-in-Publication Data

Hagland, Mark.
  Transformative quality : the emerging revolution in health care performance / author, Mark Hagland.
    p. ; cm.
  Includes bibliographical references and index.
  ISBN 978-1-4200-8492-4 (hardcover : alk. paper)
  1. Medical care--United States--Quality control. 2. Medical errors--United States--Prevention. 3. Medical care--United States--Safety measures. I. Title. II. Title: Emerging revolution in health care.
  [DNLM: 1. Quality of Health Care--trends--United States. 2. Medical Errors--prevention & control--United States. 3. Safety Management--trends--United States. W 84 AA1 H145t 2009]

RA399.A3H34 2009
362.1028'9--dc22   2008027759

Visit the Taylor & Francis Web site at
http://www.taylorandfrancis.com

and the Productivity Press Web site at
http://www.productivitypress.com

For John and for Yazmin

Contents

Acknowledgments.. xi

Foreword.. xiii

Introduction—The Quality Journey Ahead: As Pioneers
Step Out, Transformative Quality Becomes Real xv

Chapter 1 The Quality Revolution: First Steps on a Journey of
1,000 Miles 1

Chapter 2 What Purchasers and Payers Want: Value (Reliability,
Safety, Accountability, Transparency)—and Why
They're Not Getting It...15

Chapter 3 Transformative Quality: Its Context, Imperatives,
and Prospects 31

Chapter 4 Case Studies 1 to 3: Putting Patient Safety and Quality
Transformation at the Core of Clinical Operations 45

Case Study 1   Brigham and Women's Hospital: Patient
Safety and Quality Transformation at
the Core of Clinical Operations..................... 46

Case Study 2   Seven San Francisco Bay Area
Hospitals Pierce the Fog around
Medication Administration Errors............ 54

Case Study 3   Children's Hospital of Wisconsin
Exemplifies Pediatric Hospital
Innovation 60

Chapter 5 Case Studies 4 to 6: Breakthroughs in Evidence-Driven Quality and in Clinical Decision Support for Improved Care 65

    Case Study 4   Geisinger Health System's Industry Breakthrough on Quality and Transparency 66

    Case Study 5   Groundbreaking Interoperability Gives UPMC Physicians a Unified View of the Patient Record 73

    Case Study 6   Northwestern Memorial Hospital Clinicians Tackle an Array of Quality Challenges 77

Chapter 6 Case Studies 7 to 9: Initiating Transformation on a Vast Scale 87

    Case Study 7   Trinity Health Initiates Transformation on a Vast Scale... 88

    Case Study 8   Improving Stroke Outcomes in Rural Health Care Markets......................98

    Case Study 9   Tallahassee Memorial: Dramatic Improvements in Mortality Rates, Plus Transparency for the Community.............102

Chapter 7 Case Studies 10 to 11: Creating Clinical Cultures of Partnership 109

    Case Study 10 The University of Rochester Medical Center's ED Clinical Pharmacy Program Reduces Medication Errors........109

    Case Study 11 Wheaton Franciscan Healthcare Creates a Culture of Partnership...............113

Chapter 8 Change Facilitator: Information Technology and the Pursuit of Quality Transformation......................................121

9   Working Conceptually: The Use of Performance
Improvement Methodologies in Transformational
Work 139

10   Policy Considerations and the Future of
Transformative Quality 153

About the Author 159

Index 161

Acknowledgments

Many people have been truly helpful in the preparation of this book. Among them: the executives, clinician leaders, and support staff at all the organizations whose stories I told in my case studies—Brigham and Women's Hospital, Boston; the Integrated Nurse Leadership Program and the UCSF Center for the Health Professions, San Francisco; Children's Hospital of Wisconsin, Milwaukee; Geisinger Health System, Danville, Pennsylvania; the University of Pittsburgh Medical Center; Northwestern Memorial Hospital, Chicago; Trinity Health, Novi, Michigan; the Medical College of Georgia, Augusta, and REACH Call, Inc., Augusta; Tallahassee (Florida) Memorial Hospital; the University of Rochester (New York) Medical Center; and Wheaton Franciscan Healthcare-St. Joseph, and Wheaton Franciscan Healthcare, both Milwaukee, Wisconsin.

In addition to all the interviewees who are named in the case studies and in the contexting chapters of this book, all of whom were exceptionally generous with their time and their insights, and all of whom I thank as a wonderful group of industry pioneers and leaders, I want to single out for thanks the following individuals whose names do not appear elsewhere in this book, but who helped make it possible: Justin Walden and Patti Urosevich of Geisinger Health System; Corinna Kaarlela of UCSF Medical Center; Ilan Freedman and Belinda Eliahu of dbMotion, and Brian Parrish of Dodge Communications; Amy Dobrozsi, Kimberly Arndt, and Allison Richard of Northwestern Memorial Hospital; Kevin DiCola and Carol Tingwall of Trinity Health; Sandeep Agate of REACH Call and Linda Healan and Betsy Harter of Healan PR; Lori Barrette of the University of Rochester Medical Center; Rachel Stiles of Tallahassee Memorial Hospital; and Anne Ballentine of Wheaton Franciscan Healthcare.

I also want to thank my editor at Productivity Press, Kristine Rynne-Mednansky, and my publisher at Productivity Press, Maura May, for their support, encouragement, and patience. Without them, this book definitely would not have come into being. I also want to thank Jeffrey C. Bauer, PhD, my co-author on *Paradox and Imperatives in Health Care*, for his continued interest in and support of my work.

Writing a book is a fascinating venture, at times a solitary affair, yet at other times, intensely collaborative. No author is an island, and every author should express gratitude for the village of people who have made his or her book possible. Thank you all!

Foreword

Hospitals, medical groups, and other health care delivery organizations can no longer pay lip service to the quality of the services they provide. A significant group of prominent payers and empowered patients has passed a momentous tipping point, moving from tacitly accepting whatever care they received to actively expecting care that meets predetermined standards. Value-based purchasing is gaining significant momentum as more and more consumers demand proof that they are receiving top-quality medical services in exchange for their health care dollars.

Although few providers have yet been forced to make quality the number one measure of the way they do business, nearly all now recognize quality as a critical success factor for the not-too-distant future. The marketplace's initial "carrot" to promote quality, pay-for-performance reimbursement, is already mutating into an unforgiving "stick" of non-payment for non-performance. All providers worthy of their licenses must begin responding to consumers' demands for quality care as a matter of professional obligation and economic survival.

Any leader of a health care delivery organization knows that putting the theory of quality into everyday practice is much easier said than done. He or she also knows the value of learning lessons from peers who have already operationalized quality in their enterprises. This book by Mark Hagland is an essential guide for those who are ready to take necessary steps to eliminate the embarrassing and wasteful lapses in quality that have been tolerated in the past. The future will not be forgiving, and this book has a wealth of practical information about preparing for success under these new circumstances.

I am especially pleased that Mark Hagland has taken the time to expand the scope of his new work well beyond the case studies that he created for our jointly authored book, *Paradox and Imperatives in Health Care: How Efficiency, Effectiveness, and E-Transformation Can Conquer Waste and Optimize Quality* (Productivity Press, 2008). The specific purpose and structure of our work did not allow us to include all the valuable information he collected from interviews and site visits conducted to support the "big picture" perspective of *Paradox and Imperatives*. He has performed an extremely valuable service by updating a few of the previously published program descriptions and developing a robust array of new case studies from organizations that have already put the principles of quality transformation into practice.

In *Transformative Quality: The Emerging Revolution in Health Care Performance*, Mark Hagland provides the how-to details for health care executives who are ready to lead meaningful supply-side responses to the growing demand for safe and error-free medical services. Our previous book made the case for transformation and introduced structural approaches for getting started on the road to success. His new book provides detailed instructions for completing the journey.

If *Paradox and Imperatives* were a successful movie, *Transformative Quality* would be the "must see" sequel. This second work in the series has great scenes that had to be cut from the first work to keep it at a reasonable length, plus considerable new content that enriches the original. Like any good sequel, this book builds on its predecessor, but it also stands on its own. The pages that follow provide an informative and helpful picture of the best practices in health care delivery for the 21st century. The rich content shows that quality is not just a matter of life and death—it's more important than that.

This book is essential reading for all executives and managers who realize that their job is to provide Americans with the safe and effective care demanded in a consumer-directed marketplace. It shows how theory has been put into practice by some of the best delivery organizations in the world—American health systems that are setting the standards for world-class care. I recommend *Transformative Quality* without reservation for health care's leaders who know what needs to be done but need some instructions on how to do it.

Jeffrey C. Bauer, PhD
Partner, Futures Practice
Affiliated Computer Services Healthcare Solutions
Chicago, Illinois

Introduction

THE QUALITY JOURNEY AHEAD

As Pioneers Step Out, Transformative Quality Becomes Real

Every day in America, dedicated physicians, nurses, clinical pharmacists, and other clinical professionals save and improve countless thousands of patients' lives as they apply their clinical knowledge to a vast range of patient conditions, in hospitals, clinics, and other patient care organizations. They use their experience, expert clinical judgment, and collaboration with clinician colleagues to diagnose a bewildering array of medical conditions. What's more, U.S. clinical professionals are among the best trained in the world, and benefit from the availability of medical technology that is among the most sophisticated on the planet.

Yet at the same time, patients die or are injured every day because of frighteningly simple lapses in patient care quality and safety, many of which have been understood as system problems for decades. The resident who inserts a central-line catheter into a patient's side without washing his hands; the physician who hastily and illegibly scribbles a prescription for a drug whose name looks like several other very different drugs, and whose order is then misread as it is filled; the nurse who is distracted while administering medications and gives to one patient a drug meant for a different patient; all these are examples of preventable medical errors that happen in hospitals and other organizations every day.

All of these incidents occur despite the intelligence, expertise, and dedication of individual clinicians. They also happen far more often than the public ever realizes, largely because so many "near misses" are caught at some point in the care delivery chain, while many medical errors are either not understood as having taken place, or are quietly covered up. Indeed, after the Institute of Medicine stated in its groundbreaking November 1999 report *To Err Is Human* that perhaps 98,000 preventable medical errors occurred every year, many industry experts were quick to assert that that estimate was probably too conservative.[1]

The reality is that the U.S. health care system has a serious quality and patient safety problem, and has had one for a long time. Only now, as greater transparency is forced upon the system by the demands of purchasers and payers for clinical outcomes reporting and the imposition of pay-for-performance programs; and as patient care organizations themselves begin to approach the problem in a systemic way, is the profundity of the issue coming to full light.

It's All About Systems Thinking

So, as is often asserted, the United States has many of the best-trained and most expert physicians, nurses, and other clinicians in the world, why is it that our system remains sub-optimal when it comes to patient care quality and safety? To understand that fundamental issue, one must go back and look at how our health care system—which many refer to as a "non-system"—has evolved.

In Europe and America, early hospitals were sponsored either as charitable organizations run by religious denominations, or, eventually, as public institutions, run primarily by city and county governments (with some hospitals being created on for-profit or specialized-care models in the past few decades). The nature of the work on the administrative side of health care tended to encourage a custodial management style rather than an entrepreneurial one, and that environment continues to this day at most organizations. Meanwhile, physicians were trained—and still are, to the most extent—to think and work independently as clinicians. What's more, the vast majority remain independent businesspeople who are not salaried employees of hospitals. At the same time, doctors make most of the core diagnostic and treatment decisions, which are followed up by nurses, physician assistants, and other clinicians, who usually are hospital or clinic employees. Is it any wonder that incentives have not evolved in a naturally aligned way?

One additional factor has been the fact that hospitals and physicians have essentially been paid for volume of procedures, on a piece-work basis. In other words, apart from the threat of medical malpractice litigation or the occasional fraud prosecution for actual fraudulent medical claims, hospitals and physicians have been paid in full for services rendered, no matter what the outcome.

Opening Up the "Black Box"

In my public speaking presentations, I often talk about the oft-cited notion of what I call the "black box of clinical care." This means simply that until recently, it was well-nigh impossible for the public, or really just about anyone not standing directly behind a clinician giving a patient care, to find out anything meaningful or significant about the quality of that care, unless a total catastrophe led to a medical malpractice suit or some kind of official investigation. The relative quality outcomes of individual physicians, of hospitals or medical groups, remained shrouded in a fog of non-information, non-data, and a total lack of transparency overall. That box is beginning to break open now, with tremendous implications for the future of hospitals, health systems, and the clinicians and non-clinicians in those organizations.

Indeed, in the past decade, the entire operational landscape of health care has begun to shift. With health care costs exploding, the employers who purchase health care and who use health insurers as their payer proxies, as well as the federal government and state governments as purchasers, have become impatient with the value they're receiving for monies spent on health care, and have demanded change. En masse, purchasers and payers are insisting not only on improvement in quality, but the documentation of outcomes and of quality improvement. What's more, new concepts about care delivery and accountability have begun to filter into the health care industry, some of them derived from other industries. At the same time, pioneering health care organizations have begun to seriously apply performance improvement methodologies such as Lean management, the Toyota Production System, Six Sigma, and others, to clinical care delivery, with astonishing results. As a result, concepts that came out of auto and industrial equipment manufacturing, already having been applied to such service industries as financial services and transportation and hospitality, are flooding into health care, with results that are making even die-hard skeptics sit up and notice.

At the core of all this change is a concept that has taken a very long time to infiltrate health care: "system-ness." As stellar as individual clinicians can be and are in their care of patients, the health care industry is finally realizing on a mass scale that individual efforts are no longer sufficient. Instead, clinicians and non-clinicians in every patient care organization in the country must change how they deliver care as an organization, and must improve its clinical quality, patient safety, reliability, accountability, and transparency.

This required shift to system-ness means a concomitant shift to systems thinking as well. Put bluntly, hospitals and other patient care organizations—but especially hospitals—will no longer be judged solely on the skills of their clinicians, nor on all the individual fragments or elements of care delivered to patients, but increasingly, based on broader assessment of their care quality, safety, and reliability.

Fortunately, the tools of automation are finally beginning to really blossom in health care. Indeed, the implementation of key clinical information systems in hospitals and medical groups is providing a level of facilitation of process change that could not have been imagined even a few years ago. Electronic medical record/electronic health record (EMR/EHR), computerized physician/practitioner order entry (CPOE), pharmacy, electronic medication administration record (eMAR), picture archiving and communications system (PACS), and other advanced clinical systems, combined with robust data warehouses and business intelligence, predictive analytics, and other tools, are making possible objective, evidence-based, data-driven, and technology-facilitated changes that were simply not feasible or sustainable on any scale even a few years ago.

When combined, the use of performance improvement methodologies and the tools of automation together (both for care processes and for analysis and closed-loop feedback and improvement) is having an enormous impact in the leader organizations in quality and patient safety. As many of the case studies in this book (pp. 43–117) attest, there is power in organized approaches to improvement.

But there is a third factor that is turning out to be vital here, and indeed, the "spark" factor that is moving those pioneer organizations forward, and that is the emergence of a cadre of executives and clinicians (including CEOs, COOs, CMOs, CNOs, CIOs, chiefs of medical staffs, and so on, as well as exceptional leaders on the boards of hospitals and health systems) committed to fundamentally changing the quality profile of their organizations. Without that commitment, sustained over time, the transformation of quality in patient care organizations is not possible.

And it is that transformation that is the subject of this book. Throughout the book, I will be using the terms "transformative quality" and "quality transformation" to refer to broader, systemic, and organization-wide efforts to improve quality and to think systemically about quality and to act on such thinking. I use those terms to distinguish these efforts from earlier, more piecemeal efforts to improve quality. Many of those efforts, usually launched under the banners of totally quality management (TQM) or continuous quality improvement (CQI), were extremely well-intentioned, but ultimately ran aground because they lacked broad vision, executive management and board support, funding, and sustained commitment.

This book's purpose is two-fold: first, to put the growing movement towards broad quality transformation in health care into context, especially with regard to hospital organizations, where care process complexity and the potential for patient harm are greatest; and second, to describe and examine the successes to date of some of the transformative quality pioneers making waves in the industry. The fact that those pioneer organizations are making real, documented progress in changing the internal-organizational landscape of care quality and patient safety not only demonstrates that success in this area is possible; it also serves as a mirror, reflecting back on the rest of the health care industry, and implicitly challenging the vast majority of hospital-based organizations that have not yet committed to the transformative quality journey to begin to do so.

But the first fires of real change have been ignited. As more patient care organizations than one might think are making the commitment to fundamentally change patient care processes and optimize clinician workflow, to peer under the rocks of any organization's operating processes and dare to take things apart and put them back together again. And that very fact is, fortunately, reshaping the landscape of health care.

Will the quality journey ahead be difficult? Absolutely. Will many organizations stumble and fail, perhaps many times, before they achieve success? Most definitely. But if a single thing is clear, it is this: The stakeholder groups around health care—public and private employer-purchasers, health insurer-payers, and ultimately, awakened consumers—will collectively refuse to ever go back to "the black box of clinical care" as a way of purchasing, paying for, consuming, and evaluating patient care services. While still in its infancy, the transformative quality revolution is, out of necessity, here to stay. The challenge for every patient care organization in health care will be how to respond to the massive call for change—but no longer whether to do so.

NOTES

1. *To Err Is Human: Building Safer Health System*. Institute of Medicine, 1999. Online summary: http://www.iom.edu/CMS/8089/5575/4117.aspx.

1

The Quality Revolution: First Steps on a Journey of 1,000 Miles

There is nothing like it in the world. That's right: The health care system in the United States, which has evolved into its present state over the past 200 years, has taken so many policy, reimbursement, and industry turns in its history that it has become truly *sui generis*, and that largely is a bad thing. Indeed, the complexity of our health care system is such that public policy PhDs have difficulty articulating how it works; and countless books, doctoral dissertations, white papers, and industry reports have been written simply to try to bring greater clarity of understanding for policymakers, academics, and the public. The mainstream news media regularly oversimplify the workings of the system, and health care consumers and patients find themselves inside a procedural Rubik's cube even when they enter the system for routine care.

More importantly, the complexity of our system reflects a confusion over goals and values within that system. Business management avatar Peter Drucker has been quoted as saying that the U.S. health care system was the most complex industry he had ever tried to understand, bar none, and that large health care organizations may be the most complex developed in human history.[1] Drucker also told National Public Radio in October, 2005, the following:

> I always ask the same three questions whether I'm dealing with a business, a church or a university. Also, whether it's American, German, or Japanese makes no difference.
>
> 1. The first question is: What is your business? What are you trying to accomplish? What makes you distinct?

2. The second question is: How do you define results? That's a very tough question, much tougher in a non-business than in a business.
3. The third question is: What are your core competencies, and what do they have to do with results?

That's all really. There is no great difference between this century and the last except there are so many more organizations today.[2]

Now, here's an obvious question: Could health care senior executives, board members, physicians, and staff members easily answer Drucker's questions with regard to their organizations? Many leaders and front-line individuals in U.S. hospitals and health systems might have great difficulty producing coherent answers, and one consistent with those their colleagues might come up with. And therein lies a large problem. Because, for all the miracles the U.S. health care system produces every single day, saving lives and improving quality of life for millions nationwide, provider organizations remain bedeviled by sets of complex, often misaligned and even contradictory incentives, and confusion over what their organizations' goals should be and how to achieve those goals.

These contradictions have been embedded in U.S. health care for many decades. But as the cost of health care has exploded in the past four decades, the questions surrounding how the health care system should operate, and under what incentives, have taken on unprecedented urgency.

By 2007, health care spending in the United States had risen to a level of 16.2% of gross domestic product (GDP) and 19% of total national government spending, while approaching $2.3 trillion in total expenditures.[3] Those figures are alarming, especially when one considers that the next-most-expensive health care systems, measured in percentage of GDP, are those of Germany, France, Austria, and Switzerland, where annual health care expenditures ran between 10.1 and 13.0% of GDP; while Canada, the United Kingdom, Australia, Norway, and Sweden, whose health care systems deliver comparable care results, spent between 8.1 and 10.0% of their GDPs on health care in 2006.

More disturbing, however, is a combination of two key factors: Health care is not only becoming too expensive as a percentage of public and private spending in the United States; it remains an area of intense dissatisfaction for the public and private purchasers and payers of health care.

Consider the following. First, the Medicare Part A Hospital Insurance fund is becoming exhausted, as reported by the federal Office of Management and Budget in late March 2008.[4] This means that the Medicare program is endangering the balance of the United States' federal budget, at a time when the nation remains embroiled in costly conflicts in Iraq and Afghanistan, and, as of mid-2008, was heading into a recession.

Second, both purchasers and payers on the one hand, and consumers on the other, are expressing increasing frustration with the quality of health care in the U.S. system.

For example, a survey conducted in late 2006 by *USA TODAY,* ABC News, and the Kaiser Family Foundation found that only 44% of consumers were satisfied with the quality of health care in the United States, though nearly 90% were satisfied with their own providers.[5] Surveys such as this one underscore the widespread perception that the quality of U.S. health care is not what it should be.

In short, the health care system is at a crossroads, one that involves a true conundrum: how to optimize the quality of care being provided in a system that is so complex that it can be difficult just to figure out what its "levers" are, let alone how effectively to pull them. In survey after survey and poll after poll, the purchasers and payers of health care and the consumers of health care agree that the quality of care being provided needs to be improved; and further, the purchasers and payers argue, there is a distinct lack of value for monies spent. The news media also continue to report and uncover stories that underscore how much must change in health care; while those in provider organizations cringe at the coverage and the poll findings and often sit back and lament that nothing can be done.

But the vulnerability of the system to criticism is exposed whenever high-profile incidents occur, such as the heparin overdosing of the twin babies of the actor Dennis Quaid and his wife Kimberly Buffington at Cedars-Sinai Medical Center in Los Angeles in November 2007, which got tremendous media attention. Obviously, Quaid's celebrity status helped the case to garner attention. But the celebrity of the babies' parents also gave the story "legs," as they say in the news media; and additional journalistic reporting connected the Quaid twins' case with a number of other cases, including six cases that had occurred at an Indiana hospital the same year (in which three of the premature infants died) that had involved the same labeling/identification issue with the same medication.

Another recent incident illustrates the stark light in which medication errors can be portrayed in the news media when they lead to devastating consequences. In that case, a February 18, 2008 segment of the ABC News program "Nightline" told the story of the tragic death in November 2006 of Alyssa Shinn, a 14-weeks-premature infant being cared for in the NICU at a Las Vegas hospital. As "Nightline" correspondents Chris Bury and Deborah Apton reported, three-week-old Alyssa was mistakenly given, not the intravenous dose of 330 micrograms of zinc that a doctor had ordered as a nutritional supplement, but instead, 330 milligrams of zinc, a dosage that killed the tiny infant.[6] The clinician who made the initial mistake, the lead pharmacist on duty the night of the adverse event, took responsibility for the baby's death, but also noted that the nurses on duty that night should have noticed the huge size of the bag compared to the infant; indeed, she said in sworn testimony at an investigative hearing, the nutritional bag would have been four times the infant's size. What's more, "Nightline" reported, "The investigation [into the death] revealed that a series of safeguards simply failed. Two other pharmacists neglected to check [lead pharmacist] Goff's calculation. A safety stop on the mixing machine had not been set, and a technician reading the order had replenished the machine 11 times with zinc; using 48 vials of zinc to fill the baby's TPN bag. Nurses didn't notice that the nutrition bag was much larger than normal."

ONE IN 15 CHILDREN HARMED BY ADVERSE DRUG EVENTS

The significance of these incidents was reinforced by an important study whose results were released in April 2008. In the article "Development, Testing, and Findings of a Pediatric-Focused Trigger Tool to Identify Medication-Related Harm in U.S. Children's Hospitals," by Glenn S. Takata et al., in *Pediatrics: The Official Journal of the American Academy of Pediatrics*, researchers found that "Review of 960 randomly selected charts from 12 children's hospitals revealed 2388 triggers (2.49 per patient) and 107 unique adverse drug events. Mean adverse drug event rates were 11.1 per 100 patients, 15.7 per 1000 patient-days, and 1.23 per 1000 medication doses."[7] In other words, one out of every 15 children falls victim to an adverse drug event in a children's hospital (general adult hospitals were not studied). The authors' conclusion? "Adverse drug event rates in hospitalized children are substantially higher than previously described."

This 1-in-15 statistic could become the 2008 version of the oft-quoted statistic from the Institute of Medicine's groundbreaking November 1999 report, *To Err Is Human*, which found that between 44,000 and 98,000 lives are lost per year in U.S. hospitals as a result of medical errors.[8] Since then, some industry experts have argued that, based on the methodology used in that report, the actual numbers could end up being far higher than was estimated in *To Err Is Human*.

Sadly, many clinicians and other professionals in the nation's hospitals would concede that, while the fatal result in the Shinn case remains mercifully exceptional, patient safety breakdowns that lead to non-fatal injuries (as in the Quaid case) or near misses are frighteningly common nationwide. The simple question is: When and how can the overall quality and patient safety of the U.S. health care system be lifted to a reliably high level?

A CROSSROADS FOR QUALITY

The fact is that the underlying landscape around quality issues has been shifting significantly in the past few years. Indeed, the discussion around quality has been reframed, as part of a larger shift around the idea of "value" in health care. Employers and the federal and state governments, who purchase and pay for most health care in the United States, are no longer willing to accept the status quo of lack of accountability for quality, or for that matter for price and service, either.

Yet leaders of provider organizations, faced with straitened reimbursement and multiple pressures on operations, have complained that all the mandates and demands are falling on them, without the requisite resources to do what may be needed to correct the problems.

At a policy level, the political reality for hospitals, physicians and physician groups, and health systems is that there will never be a significantly larger pool of money from which to draw in order to transform the quality, patient safety, and service of the health care system. Instead, as my co-author Jeffrey C. Bauer, PhD, and I argued in the book that immediately preceded this one, *Paradox and Imperatives in Health Care: How Efficiency,*

Effectiveness, and E-Transformation Can Conquer Waste and Optimize Quality, the leader organizations in the industry are already moving forward with change, and are further compelling their peer organizations to move forward with them, or become hopelessly left behind:

> Partisan gridlock and more pressing financial obligations will prevent governments from solving the problems. Likewise, the health care industry itself will not produce timely solutions due to its internal divisions, intense competition, and related issues of antitrust law. Providers waiting for someone else to give them a fair and fast financial fix only delude themselves because almost all consumers with financial resources can go elsewhere for their health care. Clearly, the limited success of collective efforts to improve quality over the past 40 years suggests that hospitals and medical groups will need to become effective on their own, one provider at a time.
>
> ... Therefore, health care's "take-home" lesson from other industries is that organizations must implement specific production processes in order to meet predetermined criteria of effectiveness and other performance indicators established by regulators or the marketplace ... Understanding and applying this lesson is one of the most important contributions that a trustee or senior executive can make to a successful future for his or her organization. Setting and meeting objective measures of performance is the key to survival in the merging medical marketplace where nobody is willing to pay more for what they get and everybody can go somewhere else for what they want.[9]

In other words, the health care system has been launched, willing and ready or not, onto a long, complicated journey towards quality transformation, one with a very broad bell curve of journeying organizations, from the boldest pioneers to organizations whose leaders have not yet even fully realized what is happening in the industry. I will discuss in depth my definition of the term "transformative quality," which I am using throughout this book, in Chapter 3 (pages 29–42). The term is not original to me, as others have been using it recently. But it is one whose meaning, as I interpret it, is at the heart of this book—and that is, work that aims to transform the ways in which patient care is delivered, to revolutionize its levels of quality, patient safety, reliability, efficacy, and effectiveness. It is a concept that stands in stark contrast to the fragmented, bite-sized earlier attempts to improve very small aspects of care delivery, in very incremental ways.

In any case, what is fascinating about the present moment is the degree to which this "innovation gap" is present and visible. As the leaders of the most boldly pioneering patient care organizations steam ahead, the majority of hospital-based organizations remain behind the curve on quality and patient safety transformation and are either struggling to catch up with the leaders along the bell curve or are not even trying.

The leaders of patient care organizations that have done very little or nothing to move forward on health care's journey of quality transformation might do well to heed the words of the Roman orator Seneca, who two millennia ago said: "The gods guide those willing to change; those unwilling, they drag."

PIONEERS ARE MOVING FORWARD

Still, a growing number of quality pioneer organizations are moving rapidly to transform their clinical care and service quality, as well as their transparency, and to enter the emerging new world of health care value. Their leaders have made intense commitments to changing how they deliver care and to offering improved patient care quality, patient safety, service and satisfaction, and transparency, for patients, families, and purchasers and payers. Consider the following examples, described in far greater detail in the case study chapters in this book:

- So much concentrated quality improvement work has been taking place at Brigham and Women's Hospital in Boston that several years ago, executive and clinician leaders agreed that the organization should help channel its energies and efforts through a coordinating office, which in 2000 was inaugurated as the Center for Clinical Excellence. The center is an umbrella organization that is spearheading large numbers of coordinated efforts to transform the hospital's care delivery. Among the many innovations taking place, the hospital's leaders several years ago created an integrated Patient Safety Team; and have initiated a groundbreaking concept called Patient Safety Leadership WalkRounds™, in which, once a week, every week, a core group of senior executives conducts weekly visits to different areas of the hospital, joined by one or two nurses and other staff in the area, and engages the staff in that area in a discussion of adverse events or near misses that might have occurred, and about the factors or systems issues that might have led to those events. The core group includes the physician director, a patient safety manager, a pharmacist, a project manager, and a research assistant. That core group is accompanied by at least one hospital senior executive from the senior leadership team that includes the CEO, COO, CMO, CNO, and CIO. The WalkRounds™ concept, reports Michael Gustafson, MD, Brigham and Women's vice-president for clinical excellence, has become a multidisciplinary patient safety best practice among quality-pioneering hospitals, and is now spreading to hospital organizations nationwide.

- Leaders at Trinity Health, an integrated Catholic health system based in Novi, Michigan, but which serves patients in 44 hospitals across seven core, states are attempting one of the broadest quality transformation efforts to date in the U.S. health care system. Among the many elements in the initiative are the development of standardized, evidence-based order sets, in a growing range of clinical areas; the development of standardized clinical process workflows in a number of areas; the development of a standardized approach to the measurement and evaluation of pain in post-hip and knee replacement patients and in inpatients in general; the training of large numbers of clinician leaders, executives, and managers in Lean management and Six Sigma principles and strategies, in order to create a learning organization and internally develop a corps of change agents system-wide; the system-wide forward advance of a core electronic health record (EHR) for all facilities, as a key facilitator for process improvement, care quality enhancement, and patient safety; and the use of a spring forward-type approach, in which successful quality initiatives at individual hospitals within the system are then adopted system-wide, thus leveraging the work of clinician and staff leaders at individual organizations within the system.

- One of a number of hospitals receiving a Pursuing Perfection program granted by the Boston-based Institute for Healthcare Improvement, Tallahassee Memorial Hospital became one of the more noteworthy quality turnaround stories among that group. Spurred on by the revelation of sub-optimal mortality rates compared to those of other grantee hospitals in the program, clinician leaders and executives at the 770-bed community hospital have dramatically reduced overall mortality rates at their organization. In fact, within three years of working to reduce overall mortality rates, Tallahassee Memorial Hospital clinicians were able to reduce their overall rates by an impressive nearly 31%. Among the numerous areas Tallahassee Memorial clinicians have tackled collaboratively have been improvement in "door-to-dilation" for heart attack patients and the implementation of rapid response teams to address potential impending stroke situations among med-surg patients.

- Utilizing grant funding from a regional foundation, seven San Francisco Bay area hospitals used previously developed best-practice protocols for medication administration, and, after extensively training nurses and other clinicians, were able to improve medication administration accuracy among the group of seven hospitals from a baseline rate of 83.8% at the start of the program to 93.0% after 18 months. Among the critical success factors that leaders of the program cited were the empowerment and training of floor nurses, the application of systems thinking and concepts from other industries to the medication administration process, and strong adherence to consensus-driven best practices in the medication administration area.

What do these case studies (see pages 43–117 for all case studies in this book) and many others emerging in hospital-based organizations say about the state of the transformative quality journey? Simply this: Quality transformation is possible, doable, and already being done.

Significantly, the clinician and executive leaders interviewed for this book, while working on a cornucopia of different kinds of transformative quality efforts, described certain common characteristics that all their pioneering organizations appear to share. Among them:

- The initiation of the quality journey came about through stand-up leadership on the part of senior clinicians and executives in each organization. Personal leadership was at the core of the initial commitment to quality transformation. In other words, one individual or a group of individuals "stepped up to the plate" as a first step on the journey, and championed the cause of transformative quality to their colleagues and "preached the gospel" of organizational transformation in a way that resonated through the organization.
- The executive leadership of the organization, including the CEO and the rest of the "c-suite," and the board of directors of each organization

made a loud, clear, and ultimately sustained commitment to transform patient care in the organization, in order to make it higher-quality, safer, more efficient or effective, or, usually, a combination of all of the above qualities.

- Of course, it goes without saying that if an organization wants to change patient care processes, clinicians, who are the ones delivering patient care, need to be at the center of making clinical changes. And of course, that includes nurses. Researchers at the Washington, D.C.-based Center for Studying Health System Change (HSC) found in a recently released study that "[A]s hospital participation in quality improvement activities increases, so does the role of nursing." Respondents to the study's survey "reported that nurses are well positioned to serve on the front lines of quality improvement since they spend the most time at the patient's bedside and are in the best position to affect the care patients receive during a hospital stay," the study's authors further found. "As one hospital CNO noted, 'Nurses are the safety net. They are the folks that are right there, real time, catching medication errors, catching patient falls, recognizing when a patient needs something, avoiding failure to rescue.'" The study, released as an issue brief by HSC in March 2008, found that involving nurses in the multidisciplinary work necessary to effect quality transformation has been a key factor in transformative quality successes.[10]

- The leaders of each organization created a "learning culture" in the organization, investing in the resources (including education and training) necessary to spread this culture of learning across the entire organization. Key tenets of any learning culture include openness, an investigative stance, and shift away from personalization and blame and towards collaboration, systems thinking, and group problem solving. Learning-culture organizations also celebrate gains, and every organization whose leaders were interviewed for this book reported that its leaders and staff celebrated advances, especially early gains, as they moved into their quality journey.

- Those organizations that are working on broad quality transformation inevitably turn to performance improvement methodologies, including Lean management, Six Sigma, Toyota Production System, PDCA (plan, do, check, act), and a variety of other methodologies, or some combination of methodologies, in order to achieve broad and sustained gains. Transformational leaders generally agree that quality efforts will peter out quality in organizations that attempt to create broad change without the use of intelligent strategies. These methodologies, all of which have been coming into health care from other industries (especially, originally, from manufacturing), have been proving themselves in health care as they have in auto manufacturing, transportation, and hospitality services, as useful sets of tools that can take organizations places they want to go.

- One critical success factor among pioneer organizations that ties into the two previous has been is the use of data and information, and indeed, the creation of data-driven processes and organizations. In other words, personalization is taken out of discussions, and leaders and front-line clinicians and non-clinicians in pioneer organizations are agreeing to pursue change objectively.
- Pioneer organizations are also succeeding because their efforts are not only collaborative, the work is being pursued in a multi-disciplinary way. The historically ingrained divisions between and among physicians, nurses, pharmacists, and all other categories of clinicians and non-clinicians are being set aside in successful organizations, as everyone comes together to work on long-embedded problems in care delivery and other areas.
- Commitment is sustained in organizations that are making serious progress on quality transformation. Not only are the needed resources—financial, human, technological, education—being provided over long periods of time; executive management and the board in the successful organizations are publicly committing to sustained work towards change.
- Finally, pioneering organizations are pulling in all the stakeholders around them to help support and drive change—local and regional purchasers, payers, and representatives of consumer interests and the community.

INDUSTRY OBSERVERS AND LEADERS SEE CHANGE IN THE AIR

Those observing the journey (and in many cases, trying to help spur it on) see a change in the air, even compared to a couple of years ago. "I think there's a remarkable degree of convergence and awareness about what needs to happen, on a very high level; and there's an awareness that our current systems are not up to the job," says Carolyn Clancy, MD, director of the federal Agency for Health Care Research and Quality in the Department of Health and Human Services, Bethesda, Maryland. "Where we really need help is in implementation. We need systems that support the easy monitoring of quality; those systems will also support clinicians in their work. Right now," she says, "doctors and nurses are simply focused on the next patient, and oblivious to everything else, and the health care system reflects that. It's an ad-hoc-racy." Yet Clancy is heartened by the emergence of quality pioneer organizations. "No one can say there aren't good examples out there" of transformative quality success, she says. "The question is how to spread that out further across the system."

Debra Draper, PhD, an associate director at the Washington, D.C.-based HSC, says, "I would say that the majority of hospitals are aware of where we need to go. But there are only a small minority really in the lead, probably about 10% of hospital organizations. And 5 or 10% will never get there, and they probably won't be in business, to be quite frank." But the fact of the 10% of pioneers, Draper says, proves that success is possible. Draper was the lead author of the issue brief HSC published in March 2008 on the role of nurses in hospital quality improvement.[10] She says that nurses, who are pivotal to quality transformation efforts, are also "the people who face the largest number of competing priorities" on a moment-to-moment basis in their daily work in hospitals. To her, leadership from all sides is clearly critical to transforming quality. "Not just from your CEO," she adds, but from the individual staff members who are able to lead the charge and are capable of being change agents in your organization. One of the things we get at in our research brief is that they don't teach people how to be change agents and how to be comfortable in that role, in any of the professional schools. And the requirement for change is so dramatically different than it ever was, that you have to have people who are comfortable taking that leadership role and pushing things ahead."

With regard to the metaphor of the journey of 1,000 miles, Paul B. Batalden, MD, director of the Center for Leadership and Improvement and of the Dartmouth-Hitchcock Leadership Preventive Medicine Residency, at the Dartmouth-Hitchcock Medical Center in Lebanon, New Hampshire, says, "There's a lot of preparation that goes into starting the journey, and there are a lot of early experiences, and my sense is that we're somewhere between mile four and mile six" of the journey's 1,000 miles. "It's exciting, but it's really, really early. If you think about the gains being made and the celebrations we're having, they're wonderful. But this health care system is really in need of fundamental work and repair"—and that means the work will take a long time.

Moving forward, says Batalden, who is a founding member of the board of directors of the Boston-based Institute for Healthcare Improvement (IHI), "We have to understand the inextricable linkage between better patient and population outcomes with better system reform and development. It will not be sustainable on system change and performance measurement. It won't get us to the destination, because people get exhausted when you continually exhort them to do this or do that, and when you show them how their performance is mediocre. It's exhausting for the workforce. So somehow, this whole process has to recognize the inextricable linkage between better outcomes, better system performance, and better professional development."

Along the way, all those interviewed for this book agree, the leaders of patient care organizations nationwide will need to take the lessons learned from the quality pioneer organizations and leverage those lessons to try to push the health care system ahead to dramatically improve care quality, patient safety, and efficacy. What's fundamentally clear is that, though external stakeholders may help frame the discussion around this journey, and can try to push various levers to get certain results along the way, the journey will be that of provider organizations themselves to initiate, manage, and advance. In short, transformation is going to end up being self-propelled.

NOTES

1. As cited in the article "Transforming Healthcare Organizations," Brian Golden, *Healthcare Quarterly*, 10(Sp) 2006:10–19. (accessed July 2008) http://www.longwoods.com/product.php?productid=18490.
2. As posted in an online post on Scribd.com. See http://www.scribd.com/doc/263645/Peter-Drucker-quotes. (accessed in April 2008)
2. http://www.scribd.com/doc/263645/Peter-Drucker-quotes.
3. *Medical Cost Reference Guide: Facts and Trends Driving Healthcare Costs, Quality and Access*, Blue Cross Blue Shield Association, 2008.
4. "The Outlook for Medicare," *OMB Watch*, March 27, 2008. http://www.ombwatch.org/article/blogs/entry/4777/39. (accessed in April 2008)

5. Julie Appleby, "Consumer unease with U.S. health care grows," *USA TODAY,* October 16, 2006. http://www.usatoday.com/money/industries/health/2006-10-15-health-concern-usat_x.htm.

6. ABC News "Nightline": "Deadly Dose: Pharmacy Error Kills Infant." http://abc news.go.com/Health/story?id=4299616&page=1. (accessed in April 2008)

7. Glenn S. Takata, Wilbert Mason, Carol Taketomo, Tina Logsdon, and Paul J. Sharek,"Development, Testing, and Findings of a Pediatric-Focused Trigger Tool to Identify Medication-Related Harm in US Children's Hospitals," *Pediatrics: Official Journal of the American Academy of Pediatrics* 121 (2008): e927–e935. Online at: http://www.pediatrics.org/cgi/content/full/121/4/e927.

8. *To Err Is Human: Building A Safer Health System.* The Institute of Medicine, November 1999. Summary at http://www.google.com/search?hl=en&ie=ISO-8859-1&q=I nstitute+of+Medicine+report+To+Err+Is+Human. (accessed in April 2008)

9. *Paradox and Imperatives in Health Care: How Efficiency, Effectiveness, and E-Transformation Can Conquer Waste and Optimize Quality,* (Productivity Press, New York 2008), 45–46.

10. Debra A. Draper, Laurie E. Felland, Allison Liebhaber, Lori Melichar, "The Role of Nurses in Hospital Quality Improvement," Research Brief No. 3, March 2008, Center for Studying Health System Change. http://www.hschange.org/CONTENT/972/.

2

What Purchasers and Payers Want: Value (Reliability, Safety, Accountability, Transparency) — and Why They're Not Getting It

A lot of high-flown rhetoric around clinical quality and patient safety issues has been expended at health care industry conferences and by leaders of all stakeholder groups, around those issues. But what is emerging—and more rapidly than might even have been anticipated a few years ago—is a much more grounded trajectory of activity and actions on the part of purchasers and payers, and one that is leaving many hospital and health system leaders struggling to catch up to developments.

Consider the list of inpatient hospital "never events" that the federal Medicare program has announced it would no longer pay for, beginning on October 1, 2008:

- Object left after surgery
- Surgical-site infections
- Blood incompatibility
- Urinary tract infection from catheter
- Bedsores (pressure ulcers)
- Falls in the hospital

There are a few different very interesting aspects of this. First of all, this initial list (certain to be expanded over time) of so-called "never events"—incidents that simply should never happen to any patient—is very much a

"Mom and apple pie" kind of list; that is to say, it is pretty much impossible to argue with. For these kinds of errors and incidents to take place, multiple safety systems have to break down; and the regular occurrence of such events in an individual hospital would not only signal poor care quality in that facility; it would also likely trigger action by the Joint Commission or state health officials, if it became known.

More interestingly, provider executives should see the emergence of this initial never-events list from the Medicare program as, not at all an isolated development, but rather the opening salvo in the "stick" side of the carrot-and-stick efforts beginning to crest in a wave among public and private health care purchasers and payers, as they try to use whatever levers are available to them to push the health care system towards improved quality, safety, accountability, and transparency.

What's more, as everyone knows, once the behemoth Medicare program, with its annual expenditures of over $374 billion (in 2006), takes a step, private insurers quickly follow step. Indeed, within 18 months of CMS (federal Centers for Medicare and Medicaid Services) Administrator Mark McClellan's pronouncement in May 2006 that Medicare should stop paying for never events, Blue Cross and Blue Shield Association officials announced in November 2007 that their member plans would begin to phase in policies similar to Medicare's.[1] By April 2008, the Indianapolis-based WellPoint Networks had announced that it would begin denying payment for several never events—foreign objects left in patients' bodies post-surgery, pressure ulcers, air embolisms, blood incompatibility, catheter-associated urinary tract infections, vascular catheter-associated infections, and chest infections after coronary artery bypass graft (CABG) surgery.[2]

What's important here is that this is yet one more piece of evidence that purchasers and payers have begun to move forward on multiple fronts to use all the levers they can find to force quality and patient safety forward, at a time when the vast majority of hospital-based organizations still have not yet implemented systemic and systematic approaches to transforming their care quality and patient safety. As I note in the case studies that appear in Chapters 4–7 of this book (pp. 43–117), there are quality and safety pioneer hospital organizations doing just that. Yet the majority of organizations are still behind the curve. Will they catch up in time?

PURCHASERS AND PAYERS BECOMING IMPATIENT WITH PROVIDERS

There's no question that health care purchasers, and their proxies, payers, are becoming impatient with providers. After all, as health care costs and charges continue to grow far faster than inflation, purchasers are caught in a vise of conflicting demands and pressures themselves. Certainly, some core health care inflation drivers are completely outside the province of providers to do anything about, chiefly the aging of the population, and, for the most part, issues related to the explosion in chronic illness brought on in part by unhealthy lifestyles and obesity (and the issue of the extent to which physicians, nurses, and pharmacists can have any real impact on that issue lies far outside the scope of this book). But within the areas that are under providers' control—reworking their patient care processes to vastly improve quality and patient safety, not to mention accountability for outcomes and greater transparency for both outcomes quality and pricing—purchasers see too little forward movement, too late.

Indeed, in releasing the latest data on health care costs on February 26, 2008, CMS acting administrator Kerry Weems, MD, said in a statement, "The cost of health care continues to be a real and pressing concern. Making sure we are paying for health-quality health care services, not just the number of services provided, is just one of the most critical issues facing the American public and the federal government now and in the future." He added that "This projection of health care spending reminds us that we need to accelerate our efforts to improve our health care delivery system to make sure that Medicare and Medicaid are sustainable for future generations of beneficiaries and taxpayers."[3]

Among the data highlights he cited on that date:

- As a percentage of gross domestic product (GDP), the Centers for Medicare and Medicaid Services (CMS) expected health care spending to increase to 16.3% in 2007 from 16.0% in 2006. By 2017, health care spending in the United States was expected to reach over $4.3 trillion and comprise a whopping 19.5% of GDP.
- Hospital spending growth was expected to accelerate from 7.0% in 2006 to 7.5% in 2007, partly attributable to higher Medicaid payment rates.

- Growth in private health expenditures (including out-of-pocket and private health insurance spending) was expected to rebound to 6.3% in 2007 following the somewhat slower growth of 5.4% in 2006 related to the implementation of Medicare Part D. Private spending growth was expected to peak in 2009 at 6.6%, then decelerate through 2017.

The fact that the CMS administrator cited quality of care and value for money spent in releasing projections in early 2008 underscored CMS's increased interest in linking spending to quality and to value-based purchasing.

What's more, can anyone be surprised that Medicare hospital spending is in the gun-sights of Congress and policy-makers? Part A of the Medicare program (hospitals) accounts for the largest share of benefit payments out of the program (39%—see Figure 2.1 below), and Medicare spending, according to an estimate from the Office of Management and Budget (OMB), accounted for 12% for the federal budget, as of 2007.[4]

In addition, the Agency for Healthcare Research and Quality (AHRQ), a division of the Department of Health and Human Services, released

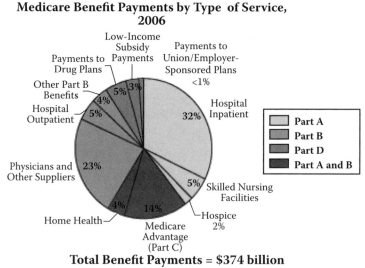

Medicare Benefit Payments by Type of Service, 2006

Total Benefit Payments = $374 billion

NOTE: Does not include administrative expenses such as spending for implementation of the Medicare drug benefit and the Medicare Advantage program.
SOURCE: Congressional Budget Office, Medicare Baseline, March 2007.

FIGURE 2.1.
Medicare payments by type of service. Source: Congressional Budget Office/Kaiser Family Foundation Medicare Spending and Financing Fact Sheet, 2007.

reports on quality and on the patient safety culture in hospitals that gave hospitals mixed grades in both areas.

AHRQ's reports reveal a split-screen landscape of quality improvement in hospitals nationwide, according to its measures.

In February 2008, the agency released its fifth annual National Healthcare Quality Report (NHQR), whose data are built on 218 measures categorized across four dimensions of quality—effectiveness, patient safety, timeliness, and patient-centeredness. The 2008 report focused on the state of health care quality for a group of "41 core report measures that represent the most important and scientifically credible measures of quality for the Nation, as selected by the HHS Interagency Work Group," according to the report.[5]

WHAT DID THE 2008 REPORT FIND?

Overall, its executive summary stated the following:

> The quality of health care in this Nation continues to improve at a modest pace. However, the rate of improvement appears to be slowing. The average annual rate of improvement reported across the core measures included in this year's fifth annual National Healthcare Quality Report (NHQR) is 2.3%, based on data spanning 1994 to 2005. An analysis of selected core measures, which cover data from 2000 to 2005, shows that quality has slowed to an annual rate of 1.5%.
>
> An important goal of improving health care quality is to reduce variation in care delivery across the country. This means that patients in all states would receive the same level of high quality, appropriate care. Since 2000, on average, variation has decreased across the measures for which the NHQR tracks state data, but this progress is not uniform. For example:
>
> • The percentage of heart attack patients who were counseled to quit smoking has increased from 42.7% in 2000–2001 to 90.9% in 2005. Moreover, 48 States, Puerto Rico, and the District of Columbia all performed above 80% on this measure in 2005.
> • Yet, in 2000, diabetic patients in the worst performing State versus the best performing state were admitted to the hospital 7.6 times more often with their diabetes out of control. By 2004, this difference had

doubled to 14. If all states had reached the level of the top four best performing states, at least 39,000 fewer patients would have been admitted for uncontrolled diabetes in 2004, with a potential cost savings of $216.7 million.

One of the key functions of the NHQR is to track the Nation's progress in providing safe health care. Five years after the first NHQR, and 7 years after the Institute of Medicine's landmark publication *To Err Is Human*, it is still difficult to document progress, although more information than ever now exists on patient safety. From 2000 to 2005, patient safety improved at an annual rate of only 1%.[6]

In other words, put very plainly, when it comes to looking down at the health care system from a 40,000-foot level, and assessing core progress towards care quality and patient safety, federal researchers see a landscape

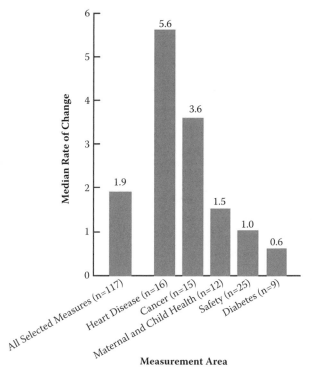

FIGURE 2.2.
Median annual rate of change in quality by measurement area, 2000–2005: AHRQ study. Source: Agency for Healthcare Research and Quality, February 2008.

of grossly uneven care quality and patient safety. This is based on rather straightforward, relatively simple measures—for example, Medicare patients about to go into surgery who have been administered antibiotics in an appropriately timed way; acute myocardial infarction (AMI) patients who were administered aspirin and a beta blocker within 24 hours of admission and prescribed aspirin and a beta blocker again at discharge, and who received smoking-cessation counseling while hospitalized; and diabetic patients who had three recommended services within the past year (at least one hemoglobin A1c measurement, one retinal eye examination, and one foot examination). Not only are all of these measures accepted as best practices across the health care industry; some of them are seen as extremely basic to core patient care competency. Figure 2.2 examines the rate of change with regard to different areas of care[7].

The AHRQ report authors do note some areas of significant improvement in the past several years on core measures, including the following:

- Over 30% more patients received appropriate timing for antibiotics before and after surgery in 2005 than in 2004.
- From 2004 to 2005, adverse drug events from warfarin and low-molecular-weight heparin declined 21% and 28%, respectively.
- Deaths following complications of care declined 2.4% from 1994 to 2004.[7]

Unfortunately, however, there is such a profound dearth of reliable data in some of these areas that:

- Only 24 of 41 safety measures in the full NHQR measure set have data available for tracking recent trends (2000 to 2005).
- No national data systems currently report data on safety at a state or local level.

In other words, there is a dearth of core capabilities to gather good data on basic quality and patient safety measures in U.S. hospitals, and it is those same capabilities, grounded in clinical information and measurement systems, which will also facilitate change and improvement in these areas. As a result, it is not inaccurate to say that, looked at from a nationwide, health system-wide perspective, work towards quality and patient safety measurement and improvement is truly in its infancy.

PUBLIC AND PRIVATE PURCHASER LEADERS' PERSPECTIVES ON THE JOURNEY OF 1,000 MILES

Is it any surprise, then, that industry observers have mixed views of quality progress on the part of hospitals and health systems to date?

Carolyn Clancy, MD, AHRQ's director, says that while she remains concerned about the lack of information and process systems to support quality measurement and reporting, the good news is that "I think there's a remarkable degree of convergence and awareness about what needs to happen, on a very high level; and there's an awareness that our current systems are not up to the job."

It will require an intensive shift towards systems thinking and towards focused improvement activity in hospitals and other patient care organizations that will move things forward, Clancy says. "Clinicians are doing the best they can, but sometimes they're colliding like atoms," she says. "We know that the task of providing health care that is reliable and that is done right every time is a team sport. In fact, a lot of errors occur because of a lack of communication. The reality," she reflects, "is that Starbucks has better system and procedure checks than most hospitals do. In addition, a lot of what used to be done in the hospital is now done in the outpatient environment, which is great, except that a lot of the people in that environment aren't doing the proper checking, and a lot of bad stuff happens. A lot of what needs to be done to make care safer and of higher quality sounds incredibly basic, but it's what we need."

Meanwhile, how far along on the quality journey of 1,000 miles do leaders in the private-purchaser (employer) sector believe hospitals and other patient care organizations have come? "Well, we're not nearly as far along as we should be, given how long we've been on it, that's number one," says Helen Darling, president of the Washington-based National Business Group on Health, and a doyenne of the purchaser world. "And in the 30 years I've been involved in it, it's as though in the first 25, we moved at a snail's pace, but we've done more in the past five years than in the previous 25." Fortunately, she says, the pace is now finally accelerating, and is eager to use whatever "levers" are available to press for more change.

"We have our four levers we can use" as purchasers, Darling says. "Number one is plan design. We're working with a group of plans and saying, we don't want you to have in your PPO and pay more to individual hospitals if an individual hospital has a poor patient safety record. Because patient safety elements such as hospital-acquired infections and serious avoidable adverse events haven't been in there, you could have a hospital that makes it on the other metrics but doesn't make it on the patient safety metrics." The challenge there, she notes, is that there is a two-to-three-year cycle for health plan contract renewals, so it takes several years to universalize any such changes.

Peter Lee, executive director of national health policy for the San Francisco-based Pacific Business Group on Health, says regarding the 1,000-mile journey of quality transformation that "The long and short answer is, we're well out of the starting gates, and the further out of the starting gates we get, not only do we have more measures and are making some progress, but we're also having a sharper view of the issues. But," he adds quickly, "what comes into sharper focus is some of the dysfunctions, when you try to do something as small as institute non-payment for errors—something that on the one hand, seems like a kind of a 'duh' kind of thing, but on the other hand, is revolutionary in health care. What would be a first baby step anywhere else is a huge leap in health care. So I'm conflicted. We've made some incredibly important steps, and have made advances in the nature of the discussion."

Lee believes that "The fact that we now have an Office of Value Purchasing in Medicare, and that Medicare has adopted the language of paying for and measuring value, and has integrated that language into its planning processes, is truly a transformative shift. The paradigm that all health care is alike, and you pay for a service, is a dead paradigm in health care. So now we recognize that there's unevenness in quality, and we shouldn't be paying for inappropriate care." Though providers are still in early stages of the journey of 1,000 miles, for the industry-leading purchaser and payer of health care services in the United States to signal a shift towards recognition of quality differentiation and towards non-payment for non-quality, Lee says, will have been seen as a turning point in the history of U.S. health care quality.

Executives at the Washington, D.C.-based Leapfrog Group, one of the organizations that has been exhorting providers on quality most loudly and clearly in the past several years, see a mixed picture among providers when they look at the nationwide landscape at this point. Karen Linscott, PT, MA, the Leapfrog Group's chief operating officer, says there are different aspects of the overall picture taking shape at present. On the plus side, she says, "The concept of transparency, which was completely in its infancy when Leapfrog started—there was no public reporting—

that is pretty much completely understood, so that's out of the gate." That said, Linscott says she continues to be disappointed both in how data are measured and reported out by providers, and by what data are measured and reported. "The speed at which information is being made available has been very slow," she says. "And it's been primarily hindered at the policy level, where the information that will be made public is being forced into the lowest common denominator, where it's not usable." Her key concern: "Hospitals have pushed the things they need to report or want to be transparent about—obviously, they need to be common, apples-to-apples measures, and that's the major value of [the measures for patient safety and care quality measured by Leapfrog's Hospital Quality and Safety Survey, including computerized physician order entry, evidence-based hospital referral, ICU physician staffing]— so the usability of the majority of the data" is extremely small.

Looking at what needs to happen in the near future, Linscott says that hospital and health system leaders need to move towards measuring and working on issues that can be made clearly meaningful to health care consumers and purchasers. "I would like hospitals to provide information that is understandable," she says. "Right now, it's things like what type of stent did you use, how many milligrams of aspirin did you provide, and frankly, I can't use those things as a consumer or as a purchaser. And until they're rolled up and aggregated, I can't reward quality differentially. And at every provider meeting I've been to, and I've been to many, many of them—the largest complaint is that we don't pay right. And we're trying to pay right. But when you look at the measures being used, they're so 'inside-baseball' that they're not usable. I don't think the data needs to be more granular— sometimes, it's overly granular—instead, it needs to be outcomes-based, understandable, and more broadly based."

Executives at research organizations have similar concerns. Maribeth Shannon, director of the Market and Policy Monitor Program, at the Oakland-based California Health Care Foundation (CHCF), says that on the one hand, "We still have a long way to go in convincing consumers that the quality of doctors' care, of hospitals' care, varies, and that tools can help them make good decisions. We have two audiences in these quality-transparency efforts. And we've been more successful with the hospitals so far—nobody wants to look bad. How does the hospital down the street compare? Nobody wants to be at the bottom. But consumers aren't there yet with transparency." On the other hand, her own organization's recent experiences with hospital quality outcomes reporting have encouraged her. "The reactions of the hospitals have been great" to the CHCF's reporting initiative, she says. "Three or four years ago, hospitals were still very reluctant to post outcomes data, feeling the data wasn't ready yet, or comparable, or whatever. But they've really come around. In fact, the fact that they were being measured in different ways by so many payers, influenced them." The CHCF has been a major supporter and funder of California's statewide provider outcomes reporting initiative, the largest in the nation (CHCF funded the initial launch of the program, which is now funded entirely by the state's leading health plans).

LESSONS LEARNED FROM THE CMS/PREMIER DEMO

Still, for all the concerns industry leaders and observers have regarding the push towards quality and towards quality measurement, there are signs of hope and change in the industry. In that regard, one series of developments that purchaser leaders from across the country are following extremely closely is the ongoing evolution of the CMS/Premier Hospital Quality Incentive Demonstration (HQID) project, sponsored by CMS and by the Charlotte, North Carolina-based Premier Inc., a national hospital alliance.

The success of the project overall, as well as the major strides in improving quality and patient safety among individual hospitals in the program, is putting the lie to the idea that financially incenting provider organizations to improve quality can't work. Consider the following:

- Hackensack University Medical Center (HUMC) in Hackensack, New Jersey, was the only hospital to place in the top decile in 10 of 15 clinical areas, and in the top two deciles in 13 of 15 clinical areas, in both years one and two of the demonstration project. Indeed, the hospital placed in the top two deciles in 10 of the 13 clinical areas in which it was eligible. HUMC also cared for more Medicare patients (2,853) over the first two years than any other participating hospital, and has received the highest total reimbursement of any hospital in the program: $1,590,000 in years one and two.
- With five participating hospitals in Iowa and Nebraska, the Alegent Health system placed in the top two deciles in 40 of 56 clinical

areas in which it was eligible over three years. Preliminary year three results show them in the top two deciles in 18 of 22 clinical areas, including top-decile placement in pneumonia at all five facilities.

- Fairview Northland Medical Center in Princeton, Minnesota, part of the Fairview Health System and one of eight Fairview hospitals participating in the HQID project, improved dramatically, moving from the bottom decile to the top decile in three of four clinical areas in which it is eligible to participate. Specific improvements have included a 61% composite quality score improvement in heart failure care and a 52% improvement in pneumonia. In addition, Fairview achieved a 100%-plus CQS score (composite quality score) in AMI treatment.

The broadest overall lesson learned from the HQID demonstration project so far is crystal-clear, says Richard Bankowitz, MD, MBA, FACP, Premier's vice-president and chief medical officer. "The first lesson learned from the project, and probably the most important one, is that if you devise a system of payment that will encourage transparency and some modest financial incentives, you can really improve quality of care," Bankowitz says. "And that's good news for patients, providers, and payers." Drilling down a level or two, he adds that, "Among the tangible lessons, one thing we've learned is that if you provide some financial incentives, you tend to motivate teamwork within an organization, because you encourage collaboration between and among the administrative and clinical staff— you bring CEOs, COOs, CFOs, CMOs, CNOs, and other executives together. What's more," he says, "these situations work with teaching and non-teaching hospitals, rural and urban, large and small hospitals, across the board. The other thing we're learning is that when incentives are aligned, improvement can be fairly rapid. We've seen fairly substantial gains in quality; and cumulatively, we've seen strong progress, but with individual hospitals improving even more rapidly. And we've also seen some narrowing of variation in outcomes; the variation has narrowed down, as the lower-ranking hospitals have moved up over three years, and that's exactly what we wanted to see."

As for the major criticism of all the pay-for-performance programs sprouting up across health care, Bankowitz says, "We always have to be vigilant about the issue of practicing to the measure. And one of the things Premier is encouraging is, rather than looking at how institutions are doing on individual measures, we'd rather measure how they're doing on a bundle of care, and IHI [the Boston-based Institute for Healthcare Improvement] also supports this—that is, if you deliver a consistent bundle of care, you're more likely to impact outcomes. So, for example, it's not necessarily the main thing that you receive the aspirin on arrival, but that you receive the full bundle of care you need. Also, performance in these areas can be surrogates for a greater overall performance going on in the hospital. For example, if you look at some of these metrics, for example, door to balloon time from ED entry to angioplasty for their emerging AMI, that is a measure that in order to do well on requires a coordination of care that even requires emergency medical services coordination, and with the cath lab staff. So that's a good surrogate for system-wide improvement."

Industry observers agree that the successes to date of the CMS/Premier HQID demonstration project are both significant and worth continuing to watch. Says Stephen Schoenbaum, MD, executive vice-president for programs at The Commonwealth Fund, New York, "I'm very optimistic overall about the progress being made" both in pay for performance and in organized quality improvement overall. "I've been writing about the results of some of these programs, but in June 2006, when Don Berwick" (IHI founder and president Donald Berwick, MD) "reported the results for the 100,000 Lives Campaign, and when the CMS/Premier demo results were reported out." Both of those things happened in that month," Schoenbaum recalls. "And I think that that really marked the turning point. Before then, most of what we were hearing was all sorts of resistance. And since then, I think there has been a much more optimistic view on the part of hospitals that they can actually do something. And I think it was a revelation to the organizations themselves that they could achieve significant results." What's beginning to happen, Schoenbaum offers, is that the mind-set of executives and leaders in hospitals and health systems nationwide is now changing towards the whole idea of the possibility of change. And that in itself is a key development.

Going forward, then, there are several key points to be made with regard to what purchasers and payers are demanding in terms of quality, patient safety, and transparency from provider organizations. To summarize:

- The era during which purchasers (both public and private) sat on the sides, passively paying for health care services without a concomitant demand for measurement, accountability, and consequences for differential care quality and patient safety, is over.

- While the quality transformation movement is still relatively new and immature, critical mass is beginning to build rapidly, in fact, more rapidly than many (perhaps most) hospital and health system leaders had anticipated.
- Early successes, such as that being enjoyed by the CMS/Premier HQID project, are quickly silencing the protests of provider executives who have in the past resisted the concepts of the imperative to fundamental quality improvement, differential reimbursement, and wide-scale measurement and comparison.
- At the same time, quality pioneer case studies emerging across a remarkable range of patient care organizations (see the case studies in this book, pp. 27–43) are adding to the rapidly growing literature of quality transformation, and further adding to the critical mass around quality transformation.

The next chapter in this book will discuss the concept of transformative quality, while subsequent chapters will examine the information technology and data challenges ahead, and policy perspectives and recommendations. What is clear, in the end, is this: The purchasers and payers of health care are through paying for patient care with no strings attached. Going forward, provider organization executives, leaders, clinicians, and staff will be challenged as never before to change how they deliver care. Those who take up the industry-wide challenge and work to become leaders in leader organizations have a relatively bright future ahead of them; those who continue to resist the wave of change face increasing struggles and woes.

NOTES

1. "BCBS plans phasing out pay for errors, 'never events.'" FierceHealthcare, Nov. 13, 2007. http://www.fiercehealthcare.com/story/bcbs-plans-phasing-out-pay-errors-never-events/2007–11–13.
2. "WellPoint stops paying for never events." FierceHealthcare, Apr. 3, 2008. http://www.fiercehealthcare.com/story/wellpoint-stops-paying-for-never-events/2008–04–03.
3. "Growth in National Health Expenditures Projected to Remain Steady Through 2017": Centers for Medicare and Medicaid Services Office of Public Affairs press release, Feb. 26, 2008. http://www.cms.hhs.gov/apps/media/press/release.asp?Counter=2935&intNumPerPage=10&checkDate=&checkKey=&srchType=1&numDays=3500&srchOpt=0&srchData=&srchOpt=0&srchData=&keywordType=All&chk

NewsType=1%2C+2%2C+3%2C+4%2C+5&intPage=&showAll=&pYear=&year=&
desc=&cboOrder=date.

4. Medicare Spending and Financing Fact sheet: Kaiser Family Foundation, June 2007. http://www.kff.org/medicare/7305.cfm.

5. "National Healthcare Quality Report 2007." Agency for Healthcare Research and Quality, Feb. 2008. AHRQ Publication No. 08–0040, p. 1.

6. "National Healthcare Quality Report 2007." Agency for Healthcare Research and Quality, Feb. 2008. AHRQ Publication No. 08–0040, p. iv.

7. "National Healthcare Quality Report 2007." Agency for Healthcare Research and Quality, Feb. 2008. AHRQ Publication No. 08–0040, p. 7.

All Web sites cited above, accessed April 2008.Chapter 3

3

Transformative Quality: Its Context, Imperatives, and Prospects

Ask anyone who has worked in a hospital-based organization for a number of years what they think of when they hear the term "quality improvement," and their minds will probably turn instantly to the total quality management (TQM) and continuous quality improvement (CQI) drives of the 1980s and early 1990s, well-intentioned efforts that inevitably found themselves boiled down, like chicken-stock reductions, to some very small initiatives indeed. Invariably chaired by low-ranking (if skilled) quality improvement departments or risk management managers or very low-ranking clinical or business office department managers, most TQM and CQI efforts in hospital-based organizations petered out over time. The key culprits? Lack of broad vision, lack of executive management and board support, the challenge of battling historic health care organization inertia, political infighting and turf battles, and most of all, the lack of a "burning platform" compelling change forward.

SO, WHAT'S DIFFERENT NOW?

During the past several years, the entire landscape around quality has shifted dramatically. The purchasers and payers of health care—and, it continues to be argued, health care consumers, though only a tiny minority have to date awakened significantly to this issue—are now demanding, very loudly, documented and rationalized value for monies spent on health care services. The news media are also increasingly becoming more interested in the issue, as more and more of the United States' GDP is spent on health care, the population ages, and issues around health insurance coverage and outcomes become increasingly prominent. Inevitably also, high-profile cases of patient care quality gone awry continue to stoke interest in quality and patient safety—or their lack—in the delivery of patient care.

Take for example the highly publicized incident that took place in late November 2007 at Cedars-Sinai Medical Center in Los Angeles. Thomas Boone Quaid and Zoe Grace Quaid, the newborn twin children of actor Dennis Quaid and his wife Kimberly Buffington, who had been born on November 8, were accidentally given massive doses of the anti-coagulant Heparin. While babies typically receive 10 units of Heparin, the Quaid twins were each mistakenly given 10,000 units each. Fortunately, quick-thinking intervention saved the twins' lives. But as reports of what had gone wrong began to surface in the news media, it became clear that a classic medication management error had taken place at Cedars. Apparently, a hospital technician had stored the Heparin in the wrong place, and a floor nurse grabbed the medicine without looking, and accidentally took out the wrong dose. Apparently, according to some media reports, as many as 13 patients as Cedars had mistakenly been given overdoses of Heparin, but obviously, the effects on the newborn twins were far more deleterious. At the same time, additional reports of similar incidents taking place with the same brand of Heparin were being uncovered, incidents that were reportedly fueled partly by the use of look-alike containers by the manufacturer.

It is incidents like these that bring to light, albeit usually in a sensationalized and fragmented way, the kinds of "near misses" that take place with regard to quality and patient safety every day in hospitals across the country.

But whereas a story like that involving the Quaid twins might have garnered considerable attention years ago, the context around such media reports has changed, at a time when quality of care and patient safety, along with value for money, are increasingly becoming mantras for health care purchasers and payers and, more and more, for increasingly sophisticated health care news media as well.

Indeed, a new "no-pay-for-errors" phenomenon began blossoming in 2007 and 2008, led by purchasers and payers of all stripes. Consider the following, from the January 15, 2008 *Wall Street Journal* article "Insurers Stop Paying for Care Linked to Errors: Health Plans Say New Rules Improve Safety and Cut Costs; Hospitals Can't Dun Patients," by Vanessa Fuhrmans:

Health insurers are taking a new tack in a bid to improve patient safety and reduce health-care costs: refusing to pay—or let their patients be billed—for hospital errors.

Aetna Inc., WellPoint Inc. and other big insurers are moving to ban payments for care resulting from serious errors, including operating on the wrong limb or giving a patient incompatible blood. The companies are following the lead of the federal Medicare program, which announced last summer that starting this October, it will no longer pay the extra cost of treating bed sores, falls and six other preventable injuries and infections that occur while a patient is in a hospital. The following year, it will add to the list hospital-acquired blood infections, blood clots in legs and lungs, and pneumonia contracted from a ventilator.

Private insurers are looking first at banning reimbursements for only the gravest mistakes. But health-insurance executives say it is only a matter of time before the industry also stops paying for some of the more common and less clear-cut problems that Medicare is tackling, such as hospital-acquired catheter infections or blood poisoning. "I'd rather have the cudgel in place first than push the list too far," says Aetna President, Mark Bertolini.

Some hospitals and [other providers, including physicians and other clinicians] are concerned that the new strategy could drive up medical costs in other ways as hospitals absorb or pass on the expense of introducing the safety and screening procedures needed to help avoid mistakes.

Ultimately, insurers say, the efforts will trigger safety improvements and savings for patients . . .

The *WSJ* article goes on to cite the errors Medicare will soon stop paying for, including:

- Object left after surgery
- Surgical-site infections
- Blood incompatibility
- Urinary-tract infection from catheter
- Bedsores
- Falls in the hospital

Further, the article notes that Aetna is beginning to stipulate in hospital contracts up for renewal that it will no longer pay, nor let patients be billed for, 28 different "never events," as compiled by the National Quality Form, a coalition of physicians, employers, and policymakers. Among these include:

- Leaving an instrument in a patient after surgery
- Death of a mother in a low-risk pregnancy
- Allowing a patient to develop bedsores
- Using contaminated devices

What is clear is that these moves on the part of the Medicare program and private health insurers are only the beginning. Over time, as the pay-for-performance movement evolves forward, no-pay-for-low-performance, as referenced in Chapters 1 and 2, will become a reality in those areas in which a clear connection can be established between clinical responsibility and discrete payment elements.

At the same time, more and more data are becoming available on a range of quality measures across the U.S. health care system, and not all the data are moving in a positive direction.

For example, a September 10, 2007 study published in the *Archives of Internal Medicine* found that the number of serious adverse drug events reported annually to the Food and Drug Administration (FDA) more than doubled from 1998 to 2005, to 89,842.[1]

During that period, Thomas J. Moore, of the Institute for Safe Medication Practices, Huntingdon Valley, PA, and his colleagues, note the number of serious and fatal adverse drug events (ADEs) reported to the FDA (1998 was the first year such reports were collected nationally) increased 2.6-fold, from 34,966 in 1998 to 89,842 in 2005, while fatal ADEs increased 2.7-fold during the same period, from 5,519 to 15,107. What's more, the authors noted, from 1998 to 2005, reported serious events increased 4 times faster than did the number of outpatient prescriptions written during that same period.

As Moore and his colleagues see it, "This study shows that substantially growing numbers of patients are experiencing serious injuries from drug therapy, although the exact magnitude of the population increase cannot be estimated from these data. Future initiatives to improve drug safety," they add, "require more accurate and capable systems to monitor postmarketing ADEs. This growing toll of serious injury shows that the existing system is not adequately protecting patients and underscores the importance of recent reports urging far-reaching legislative, policy, and institutional changes."

INCONSISTENCY FOUND NATIONWIDE

Further, even those studies and reports that are showing some improvement across the U.S. health care system as a whole are also highlighting broad-based inconsistencies in quality and patient safety.

Take for example the findings of *Improving America's Hospitals: The Joint Commission's Annual Report on Quality and Safety 2007,* released on November 12, 2007, by the Oakbrook Terrace, Illinois-based Joint Commission. While the press release for the report noted that "American hospitals are making measurable strides in the quality of care provided for patients with heart attacks, heart failure, pneumonia and surgical conditions" (with regard to aggregate performance of accredited hospitals against the organization's standardized national performance measures and its National Patient Safety Goals), the organization noted that "Whether or not patients receive proven treatments for these common reasons for hospitalization often depends on where they live. For example, statewide performance of hospitals on the measure of providing discharge instructions to patients with heart failure ranges from 49% to 91%."[2]

Among other things, the authors of the report noted "A 90% compliance level was achieved for only four of 22 quality-related measures tracked during 2006. In addition, certain treatments are not being performed consistently for some measures in place since 2002. For example, two measures introduced in 2002 that relate to prescribing of ACE inhibitors at discharge for patients with heart failure or with heart attack show the most room for improvement, with hospitals offering these treatments only 64 and 56% of the time, respectively."

The study's authors also note that "Requiring hospitals to follow standardized processes for quality measurement, reporting and improvement has contributed significantly to the positive results. For measures tracked for the first time in 2005, performance was generally lower and more variable than for measures tracked since 2002. This," the reports authors note via their press release, "demonstrates a clear correlation between performance measurement and quality improvement. Much of the improvement reflected in this report can be attributed to the consistent application of focused, evidence-based measures which are the foundation of the Joint Commission's performance measurement endeavors."

What's more, the report's Executive Summary notes, "requiring hospitals to follow a standard process for continual quality measurement, reporting and improvement has contributed significantly to this improvement. Implemented several years ago, this process requires hospitals to report quality-related performance. In turn, performance results are publicly reported through this report, the Quality Check Web site (www.qualitycheck.org) and other means."[3]

HARDER IN HEALTH CARE

If some patient care organizations are making pioneering progress in transforming their care delivery and effectiveness, while others are far behind or not yet even on the path towards transformation, there are valid reasons for the gaps and challenges.

To begin with, as I have often noted in my speaking engagements on health care policy and quality, the health care industry is going through two revolutions at once. For the first time in its history, this $2.1 trillion "cottage industry" is beginning to become systematized, as the Joint Commission and other organizations have been advocating, towards some standardization of clinical practices, while it is at the same time going through its transformation to automation, with the long-awaited transition to adopting the electronic medical record/electronic health record (EMR/EHR) and other tools that will be required to improve quality and consistency. No other industry in the United States has been required to go through its Industrial Revolution and Information Age Revolution at the same time; and the difficulties inherent in doing so are clearly manifest industry-wide. In a field where health information management (formerly medical records) professionals aren't even working from a consistent, health care system-wide vocabulary for basic procedures and treatments clinicians are using, the challenges of standardization and the elimination of unnecessary variation and the improvement of care quality are daunting.

At the same time, quality innovators in health care are having to take into account and work with the fundamental complexity of patient care delivery processes and work processes in general. Indeed, a whole new sub-industry is emerging of experts and advisers who are helping to translate such quality improvement methodologies as Lean Management, Six Sigma, PDCA, and Toyota Production System (TPS)—methods that can be applied in a very straightforward way in industries like manufacturing and transportation—into health care-specific vocabulary and methods. Numerous books, white papers, conferences, and tutorials are being created in order to make such translation possible, given the vast differences between manufacturing (where the main methodologies first arose) and the immensely complex service industry known as health care.

Such work is necessary and helpful, say those who have devoted their professional work to improving health care. "It's a very complicated industry," says James Reinertsen, MD, head of the Reinertsen Group, an Alta, Wyoming-based independent consulting and teaching practice, and a Senior Fellow at the Boston-based Institute for Healthcare Improvement (IHI). "I have a few different points of external reference for that statement," explains Reinertsen, who spent a number of years in clinical practice, as well as a decade as CEO of the Park-Nicollet Health System in Minneapolis. "Peter Drucker came late to health care, but he said once that the modern hospital is the most complex form of human organization ever created," Reinertsen notes.

And he adds another anecdote. "Once," he says, "I was in negotiations with my board about my pay," during the time he was CEO at Park-Nicollet. "And my human resources guy brought me an article from a magazine in which one fellow had created a system that rated the complexity of CEOs' jobs by industry, including manufacturing, and so on. He had normalized the degree of difficulty scale on a 0 to 100 basis. I recall that certain types of manufacturing rated around 20, and the role of a pharmaceutical CEO ranked somewhere around an 85. When we went back and put the role of a hospital CEO on the scale, the number came out to be 130. And one of the reasons is that the CEO of a modern hospital in virtually all instances has virtually 100% of his costs being determined by people who aren't employees and have no accountability to him, and that obviously makes his or her job immeasurably difficult."

REVERSING A TRADITION OF CUSTODIALISM IN HEALTH CARE

Another built-in challenge for innovators has to do with the cultural history of health care, particularly that of hospitals. In medieval Europe, early hospitals were established by communities of monks and nuns, and many were also poorhouses or hostels for religious pilgrims. Indeed, an early French term for hospital, "hotel-Dieu," translates loosely as "hostel of God." In the United States, early hospitals were either established by religious orders or by local governments. And their heritage of charity care and community-centeredness meant that hospitals were anchored firmly in the not-for-profit orbit for many decades, attracting a certain type of management and leadership, as well as offering relatively low pay compared to that offered to executives in for-profit industries. In addition, the evolution of the fee-for-service reimbursement system discouraged any innovation in patient care processes, as in fact, the system has long paid all providers and clinicians alike, rewarding not only mediocre care, but even at times substandard care.

Yet despite the built-in challenges facing any who would do transformative work in health care, significant change is taking place in our industry. True, faced with mounting evidence of the wildly uneven state of patient care quality and safety nationwide, those hospital and health system clinician leaders and executives who would see the quality glass to be half-empty might be excused for momentarily (but only momentarily) sagging in their swivel chairs, as they contemplate the vast challenges ahead.

Yet at the same time, one of the major complaints heard regularly in corridors of hospitals, medical clinics, and other patient care organizations nationwide is becoming more and more hollow in its ring, as the notion that comprehensive change cannot take place or be sustained is knocked down over and over in patient care organizations from Maine to Florida to Washington state to California.

On a broad level, the successes to date that have come out of the CMS/Premier Hospital Quality Incentive Demonstration (HQID) project, co-sponsored by the federal Centers for Medicare and Medicaid Services and Premier Inc., the Charlotte-based hospital and health system alliance, are putting the lie to the notion that widespread, significant change can't take place.

In January 2008, for example, Premier was able to publish a press release trumpeting the changes taking place among the 260 hospitals participating in that groundbreaking program.[4]

"According to the analysis" of mortality rates and costs among the hospitals participating in the program, "the broadest of its kind," the January 31, 2008 press release noted, "of 1.1 million patient records from participating Hospital Quality Incentive Demonstration (HQID) hospitals, if all hospitals nationally were to achieve the three-year cost and mortality improvements found among the HQID project participants for pneumonia, heart bypass, heart failure, heart attack (acute myocardial infarction), and hip and knee replacement populations, they could save an estimated 70,000 lives per year and reduce hospital costs by more than $4.5 billion annually," extrapolating from the results for the 8.5% of all patients nationally who received care in the HQID hospitals. "On average, the median hospital cost per patient for participants in the MCS/Premier HQID project declined by over $1,000 across the first three years of the project, whereas the median mortality rate decreased by 1.87%," the press release noted. And the feds are absolutely looking closely at the implications of such results. "Our experience with this pay-for-performance demonstration have provided us with invaluable guidance as we continue to pursue and develop value-based purchasing incentives," Kerry Weems, acting administrator for CMS, said in a statement included in that news release.

Similarly, the Boston-based Institute for Healthcare Improvement's numerous quality improvement programs are bringing more success into plain view. Among the numerous innovations the IHI has helped to spread across patient care organizations throughout the United States and internationally are such concepts as its "SBAR" (situation, background, assessment, recommendation) methodology for gathering information for clinical decision-making; the use of rapid response teams for mobilizing efforts to turn patient situations around before the condition of individual patients can deteriorate dramatically, and the use of multidisciplinary rounds to enhance communication and care planning among clinicians on patient floors.

WHAT TRANSFORMATIVE QUALITY IS

Meanwhile, whether they are involved in the CMS/Premier initiative, the IHI initiatives, another program sponsored by another group, or simply developing their improvement initiatives organically, the flowering of these transformative quality efforts nationwide (and, of course, internationally as well) is making it harder and harder for naysayers to claim that comprehensive work cannot be done.

What's more, organizations like Tallahassee Memorial Hospital are doing transformative quality work. Out of a variety of individual circumstances, *definition* (handwritten marginal note)

hospitals and other patient care organizations across the country are committing to making vast changes in their patient care processes and bringing about significant, systemic improvements in quality, transparency, and accountability. That is the core of transformative quality. Transformative quality means the strategic, comprehensive overhaul of patient care delivery and associated processes in order to create fundamental improvement in clinical outcomes, clinician and staff effectiveness and efficiency, and patient and community satisfaction. It is the opposite of a low-level, "micro" focus on very small processes or elements of care delivery, though inevitably, transformative quality drills down to very specific elements of care delivery in the work its leaders carry out to achieve their aims.

Transformative quality work is getting results in organizations of all types. The marquee result of Tallahassee Memorial's several years' worth of transformative quality work? A stunning 31% reduction in overall inpatient mortality between 2001 and 2004.

Comprehensive, transformative quality improvement is very possible, says Barbara MacArthur, RN, MN, vice-president and chief nursing officer of the 770-bed Tallahassee Memorial Hospital, the flagship inpatient facility of the integrated Tallahassee Memorial Health Care, located in Florida's state capital. Beginning with what she calls "pretty low-hanging fruit," MacArthur says that she and her colleagues began their transformative quality path back in 2001 and 2002, when they applied for a Pursuing Perfection grant from the IHI. The fact that Tallahassee Memorial started out with the highest overall inpatient mortality rate of any of the 13 Pursuing Perfection hospital organizations was a major "wake-up call" to their organization, and helped, along with strong community pressure for cultural change, to spur action, and provide the Tallahassee Memorial folks with the burning platform they needed, MacArthur recalls (see full case study, pp. 99–105).

In addition to the "burning platform for change" that is required to ignite transformative quality efforts, MacArthur says that "in all cases, leadership, cultural change, and commitment" are required for the success of any transformative quality initiative, as well as "a critical mass of strong operational people, because you may be very well-intentioned, but you need folks who can get it done."

"There's no doubt that it's hard to make change," says Alfred Casale, MD, surgical director at the Geisinger Heart Institute and the initial clinician champion for the Danville, Pennsylvania-based Geisinger Health

System's revolutionary ProvenCare program, which has created sets of best-practices clinical protocols across several different surgical areas, beginning with coronary artery bypass graft (CABG) surgery, and tied those clinical protocols to a first-in-the-nation guaranteed-price-for-surgery program. As at Tallahassee Memorial, conditions at the seven-hospital Geisinger were ripe for change several years ago. And whereas at Tallahassee Memorial, things were set in motion after a community-wide call for hospital change and a rapid turnover of most of the executive leadership of that organization, at the Geisinger organization, the unraveling of a previous health system merger coincided with a level of internal dissatisfaction and recognition of the need for change. In the case of Geisinger, the arrival of a passionate new physician CEO, Glenn Steele, Jr., MD, set off a chain of events that has transformed the organization's approach to quality. But it was Dr. Casale who first answered the call for transformation.

Importantly, every single clinician leader interviewed for this book acknowledges that leading transformative quality initiatives is challenging and difficult. Yet they universally also believe that individual leadership, backed up by executive management support and reinforced by a burning platform for change, can really catapult any patient care organization forward. "It may be a truism that one person, two people, ten people, can make change; but it's also very true," says Casale. "It's like the butterfly effect; I'm truly convinced of that. There's no doubt in my mind that a good idea, with a champion behind it who's not easily dissuaded, can lead an organization towards a tipping point" of change adoption and acceptance.

Starting out with grand plans but lack of clinician champions, or very well-thought-out specific projects, can mean doom, says Geisinger's CEO Steele. Instead, he urges, "You start with what is under your control, and what can't hurt patients, that's the first thing. And if it's benefiting patients, and you can document it in some way," that creates momentum towards change. "Demonstrating in our ProvenCare portfolio" (see pp. 64–70 for the full Geisinger ProvenCare case study) "that we can actually show improved quality that is linked to lower costs for a population of patients, is my goal here. And then others around the country will figure out how to scale and generalize programs like ours. Of course, such work," he adds, both in individual organizations like Geisinger's, and nationwide, "is the work of a lifetime."

LESSONS LEARNED BY SENIOR EXECUTIVES

What's clear even now, however, is that the work being carried out in orga-nizations like Geisinger Health System all around the country is already yielding some precious, generalizable, lessons learned.

Dr. Reinertsen says that several elements have become clear in his work. "First," he says, "hospital leaders, the majority of whom are not clinicians, have had to change their questions around getting the doctors involved. The question is not 'How can we get the doctors involved in our quality and safety agenda?' Instead, it's 'How can we get involved in the doctors' work?' Executives need to get engaged in ways that engage the hearts and minds of doctors," he urges.

Indeed, Reinertsen cites several critical elements that must be part of CEOs' and senior executives' thinking at the very outset, in order for transformative quality to ultimately manifest. Among these:

- Engage physicians and other clinicians around their biggest concerns.
- Physicians' two most fundamental concerns are improving the out-comes of their individual patients and optimizing their time and workflow.
- The entire dialogue around quality improvement and optimization must perforce take place at a systemic level, thus eliminating the cul-ture of blame and the search for "bad apples" that has until recently infected health system thinking.
- Patient safety, one of several key components of quality improve-ment, is a particularly effective rallying point for clinicians.
- Make every piece of an initiative a "win-win" for clinicians and exec-utives alike.

"It turns out that there are two fundamental concerns among doctors," Reinertsen says. "One is individual patient outcomes—what happened to my patient? That element speaks to their professional reputation, their sense of professional excellence, and their genuine caring for their patients as human beings. And the second element," he says, "is around wasting their time. Don't do that, or you won't begin to succeed. They also get hung up on anything that wastes their patients' time as well, because they're the point person for that issue. But don't ask physicians to reduce your overall institu-tional lengths of stay. They'll reject that out of hand—and I wouldn't blame them!" Instead, he says, reframe every issue in terms of patient care, and clinicians will far more easily be won over. Also of course, as was dramatically the case with regard to the successes to date of Geisinger's ProvenCare program, attracting one or a few key physician champions early on will be an absolute must-have for any quality initiative that would get at the core of patient care quality, and therefore be transformative if successful.

EARLY SUCCESSES ARE EXCITING THE FIELD

What is clear about the early successes of organizations like those that are evolving forward at organizations like Geisinger Health System and Tallahassee Memorial Hospital is that the very fact of demonstrable, documented successes taking place is helping to spur interest in tackling the challenges of quality transformation across health care, says Stephen C. Schoenbaum, MD, executive vice-president for programs at The Commonwealth Fund, New York. "I think such success has been a revelation to the organizations themselves," Schoenbaum says, referring to the significant improvements in care quality being documented by such broad initiatives as that of the CMS/Premier effort. "I'm not close enough to the IHI campaign or the Premier demo to know for sure what people said when they first signed up," Schoenbaum continues. "But I think the successes of those programs have been somewhat beyond their expectations." Indeed, Schoenbaum says, he recently had dinner with a senior executive at New York Hospital, which is now devoting weekly Friday morning programs for managers from all five system hospitals to the subject of quality and safety. His contact there, Schoenbaum says, believes that in that organization, as in many others nationwide, "A tipping point has finally occurred in the recognition of the *Crossing the Quality Chasm* report" that was published by the Institute of Medicine back in 1999. "What's clear to me as I talk with hospital executives from organizations across the country," he says, "is that the discourse around quality is really totally different from what it was five years ago."

As transformative quality continues to take hold, such shifts of perception will be important to furthering the momentum of the phenomenon. Success will breed success going forward, says Maribeth Shannon, director of the Market and Policy Monitor Program of the Oakland-based California Health Care Foundation (see pp. 24 for a description of that program). Based on her work helping hospitals across California to publish quality outcomes data and encouraging system-wide improvement and transparency, Shannon says that "I'm quite optimistic that we're making progress" towards significantly improved quality across the U.S. health care system. "I truly think that quality has improved tremendously in hospitals in the past five years, and it will improve tremendously more in the next five years," Shannon says. "I really think there's no turning back. Right now, we're still focusing on particular kinds of things we can measure; we haven't been able to roll it all up yet" into comprehensive measurements of patient care quality that can move the transformative quality phenomenon forward on a fast track. "But the concept of transformative quality is clearly where we need to get."

NOTES

1. Laurie Barclay, MD, "Reported Serious and Fatal Adverse Drug Events More Than Doubled Between 1998 and 2005," *Archives of Internal Medicine* 167, no. 16 (2007): 1752–1759. http://www.medscape.com/viewarticle/562642.
2. *Improving America's Hospitals: The Joint Commission's Annual Report on Quality and Safety 2007.* http://www.jointcommission.org/NewsRoom/NewsReleases/nr_ar_07.htm. (accessed April 2008)
3. http://www.jointcommissionreport.org/executive/executivesummary.aspx. The full report can be accessed at: http://www.jointcommissionreport.org/pdf/JC_2007_Annual_Report.pdf. (accessed July 2008)
4. http://www.premierinc.com/about/news/08-jan/performance-pays-2.jsp.

SIDEBAR 3.1

Change witness
Rethinking language

James Reinertsen, MD, of The Reinertsen Group, says:

"Administrators need to change their thinking from the old model that posits that the doctors are 'our customers' to the doctors are 'our partners'; and that is a very, very difficult thing to do. Most CEOs have written language in their organizational goals saying that their doctors are their customers. They need to elevate doctors to partners, and instead posit that their patients are the customers. We did this at Park-Nicollet" (the Park-Nicollet Health System, where Reinertsen served for a decade as CEO), "and rearticulated the concept to the idea that the patient is our only customer. This issue is really hard because it involves sharing power with the doctors. And that's a transformational, difficult change. The flip side of this coin is that doctors have to make a transformational change: they have to recognize their responsibility not only for the outcomes of the patients whom they personally see, but for the broad outcomes of the entire organization. And that's a very complicated shift for doctors—thinking in terms of system. But if you can achieve that, you can move on to strategies and then tactics."

4

Case Studies 1 to 3:
Putting Patient Safety and
Quality Transformation at the
Core of Clinical Operations

The first case study in this chapter looks at the groundbreaking work being done at Brigham and Women's Hospital in Boston, where a team of clinicians have supercharged their care quality and patient safety initiative through the creation of a Center for Clinical Excellence, a virtually unique office for quality improvement in an academic medical center (pp. 44–53).

This chapter's second case study describes the results of an innovative grant-based program that ran for 18 months in seven San Francisco Bay area hospitals and achieved impressive results in improving medication administration accuracy, through adherence to consensus-based medication administration protocols, and the empowerment of nurses (pp. 53–57).

"While the underlying quality and patient safety approaches are very similar no matter what setting patients are in, the stakes in pediatric hospitals are very high," observes Ramesh Sachdeva, MD, PhD, DBA, vice-president for quality and outcomes at the 236-bed Children's Hospital of Wisconsin, in Milwaukee. In the third case study in this chapter, Sachdeva and his colleagues talk about innovations they are bringing to fruition in the special environment of children's hospitals (pp. 57–62).

CASE STUDY 1

Brigham and Women's Hospital: Patient Safety and Quality Transformation at the Core of Clinical Operations

People in hospital organizations all around the country who would posit that transformative performance improvement in patient safety and care quality is not possible need to learn about what's happened in the past several years at Brigham and Women's Hospital (BWH) in Boston. The 747-bed academic medical center, which is in turn one part of the vast nine-hospital Partners HealthCare system, has become something of an industry beacon on the nationwide journey to transformative quality.

Indeed, so much has been going on at BWH that several years ago, executive and clinician leaders agreed that the organization should help channel its energies and efforts through a coordinating office, which in 2000 was inaugurated as the Center for Clinical Excellence. The center, led by Michael Gustafson, MD, MBA, vice-president for clinical excellence, executive director of quality and safety, has been at the heart of the work to guide BWH's quality transformation efforts ever since.

There are numerous aspects to the transformative quality work taking place at BWH, but two aspects that stand out in particular are the creation of an integrated Patient Safety Team, and the initiation and expansion of Patient Safety Leadership WalkRounds™. The WalkRounds™, Gustafson reports, have become a multidisciplinary patient safety best practice among quality-pioneering hospitals, and are now spreading to hospital organizations nationwide. Indeed, the work of the integrated Patient Safety Team has been described in a number of professional journal articles, including in the August 2003 issue of the *Joint Commission Journal on Quality and Safety.*[1]

Importantly, all these developments have arisen out of an early strategic choice about how to create and advance quality at BWH. "When we created the team back in 2000," says Tejal Gandhi, MD, executive director of quality and safety, "we made a conscious decision about where we were going to place it. We didn't want patient safety to be this sort of silo somewhere that wasn't related to any other activity," she emphasizes. "Risk management had historically done the work; quality improvement was another group that had handled such issues. And it just made sense to have the two pieces connected."

Gustafson says, "We need to emphasize that we have a Patient Safety Team, but with a lot of connections to everyone. We have 13,000 employees, and we want everyone thinking about patient safety. And with five or six people on our team, we have to leverage that." As Gustafson sees it, "We're content experts, we try to assess where the organization's major opportunities are, and help to try to leverage the major initiatives centrally."

Building a Culture of Quality by Walking Around (Together)

What Gustafson and his team have been able to leverage has been quite significant. To begin with, there are those Patient Safety Leadership Walk-Rounds™, initiated in 2001. How do those work? Essentially what happens is that once a week, every week, a core group of senior executives conducts weekly visits to different areas of the hospital, joined by one or two nurses and other staff in the area, and engages the staff in that area in a discussion of adverse events or near misses that might have occurred, and about the factors or systems issues that might have led to those events. The core group includes the physician director (Gandhi), a patient safety manager, a pharmacist, and a research assistant. That core group is accompanied by at least one hospital senior executive from the senior leadership team that includes the CEO, COO, CMO, CNO, and CIO.

What types of issues typically come up on these weekly WalkRounds™? "A really broad range of issues is uncovered," Gustafson says, "all the way from a door being open inappropriately to a nurse's having trouble identifying which physicians to page regarding specific problems." With regard to the latter challenge, he cites one example in particular of an issue that was addressed via the WalkRounds process. Because of the constantly changing medical staffing on patient floors, he says, "Nurses have had trouble identifying which physician is caring for each patient. So that's led to a project to redesign and build a new physician coverage program, which at press time was set to go live soon. When the new system is implemented," he continues, "instead of just posting which days individual physicians—primarily residents—are covering, if a physician leaves the hospital, he or she will have to assign their patients to the doctor who is covering next." This problem primarily relates to resident coverage, he notes, as each patient always has one attending of record.

Gandhi adds that "Since the imposition of the 80-hour rule" (the implementation in July 2003 of federal resident work-hours limitations based on recommendations put forward by the Accreditation Council for Graduate Medical Education), "there might be four or five residents changing coverage in a single day. We have a software program" to help manage resident hours, she notes, "but it's not granular enough to get down to the two-hour level." By 2009, the hospital expects to go live with the new computer system created to assist in managing that issue. And the questions raised regarding resident patient coverage, and its potential to create patient safety and quality issues, have been uncovered during WalkRounds.

Furthermore, Gustafson says, this weekly process is strongly abetted by a closed loop of analysis, discussion, and further action. That's what makes the whole process work, he says. "That framework" for performing the WalkRounds™ weekly "has worked well for us," he reports. "The question is, how do you find out when an adverse event occurs so that you can do an analysis and make systems changes? So you have to have really robust ways of identifying events. Two, how do you do more proactive analysis, and that's looking at best practices, doing analysis. Third, what are levers to impact the culture, with longer-term benefits? And fourth, specific activities around medication safety, since that's the biggest single area."

Much has been learned in seven years of performing the WalkRounds process, Gustafson and Gandhi agree. What's more, Gustafson says, "Being one of the first places to do this, we've established what has become a fairly standard national best practice. How do you get senior leadership to demonstrate their commitment? This always comes up as a recommendation," he says. "We've worked with two different CEOs, two COOs, two CNOs, and one CMO, and sustained the commitment of our senior leadership across seven years," he notes.

Having at least one member of the senior executive leadership team sends a signal to everyone in the hospital that this is an important element in important work for the organization, says Sue Schade, BWH's vice-president and CIO, who adds that she is a wholehearted supporter of the WalkRounds™ process, and who commits firmly to participation once a month in the process. In addition, Schade says, "issues around IT needs always come up. And," she says, "I've found that my hearing it first hand is a huge plus."

In any case, the patient safety team follows a rigorous process regarding events captured in the WalkRounds process. Such events are entered into a database and classified according to their contributing factors. The data are aggregated by contributing factors, and identified via priority scores in order to highly root issues. The priority scores are used to help develop quality improvement pilot projects and optimize the use of limited resources. And executives are surveyed quarterly about actions they've taken as a result of WalkRounds and are asked what they've learned from the rounds.

The WalkRounds process has also expanded geographically. "For the past year or two," Gustafson reports, "we've extended the program to the ambulatory area, and going out to the 12 different primary care practices and having a discussion in that setting as well; obviously, different issues come up."

For the Integrated Patient Safety Team's leaders, the WalkRounds program is far from being simply a problem-solving mechanism. Rather, they view the WalkRounds process as a mechanism for spurring organizational change and transformation. "At first," says Gandhi, "we spent most of the time on culture and on identifying and analyzing events and following up on them. Over time as those have become more robust, we've shifted more towards proactive analysis." As a result, she says, "The amount of time on various elements has definitely shifted over time."

What's more, Gustafson says, he and his colleagues have focused strongly on the particulars of patient safety and care quality in an academic environment. "We've really tried to involve residents and staff in this," he says. "In fact, we have a patient safety rotation that involves a few residents each year. Residents," he reflects, "can create challenges, as they're always rotating around different services."

The CCE and the Patient Safety Team

The WalkRounds™ program itself is of course managed by a team—the staff in the Center for Clinical Excellence who are part of the integrated Patient Safety Team. The Patient Safety Team was incorporated in May 2001, with the goal of creating the safest possible environment for patients and staff by creating a culture of safety, developing the capability to measure and evaluate processes, committing to changing processes that need to be made safer, and adopting new technologies. The team consists of a medical director, a patient safety manager, a pharmacist, a project manager, and a data manager. When the team was established, it was immediately placed into the Center for Clinical Excellence.

The team, Gandhi says, focuses in a laser-like way on the organization's key patient safety initiatives, working collaboratively with clinicians and other staff throughout BWH who are involved in efforts around safety and quality. "We've tried to maintain strategy clarity, as well as really good communication among all the groups that work on patient safety, including nursing and pharmacy," she says. What's more, the creation of the team now appears prescient, with regard to the significant increase in patient safety mandates coming out of the Oakbrook Terrace, Illinois-based Joint Commission. "Since we created the team, there have been a lot of Joint Commission mandates," she notes, "and there's a lot of required reporting of data." What's more, Gustafson says, "The annual Leapfrog Survey that hospitals complete is a real mix of quality and safety components," adherence to which requires a very focused, multidisciplinary approach, he says. "There are several components around infection control, medication safety, etc. And we have our quality and safety people take the lead in assessing the gaps. Remember, we need to emphasize that we have a Patient Safety Team, but with a lot of connections to everyone throughout the organization. We're content experts," he adds. "We try to assess where the organization's major opportunities are, and help to try to leverage the major initiatives centrally."

Among the advances created out of the development of the multidisciplinary team include:

- An inclusive, multidisciplinary approach to the process of event analysis
- The development of a comprehensive database that includes all incident report data
- The production of quarterly reports highlighting patient safety trends by severity, item and frequency, at a level granular enough to examine trends among individual services, locations, and event types
- Distribution of these reports to all committees responsible for various types of incidents and to nursing and medical leadership
- Work by the patient safety manager with the various groups to evaluate observed trends and to work further with service-based multidisciplinary improvement teams to direct appropriate interventions
- With support from the Information Systems department, development of Web-based reporting for greater efficiency and ease of distribution of such reports

Within the Center for Clinical Excellence are five sections, each with its own area of emphasis: Patient Safety, Quality Programs (whose duties include measurement of mandatory and other quality metrics and structuring improvement activities), Performance Improvement (whose internal consultants work on patient flow, satisfaction, and operational efficiency issues), Decision Support (which helps to manage the organization's data for internal reporting and analysis), and Financial Analysis and Planning (which was added four years ago). What's important regarding these specialized capabilities, Gustafson says, is that "We have the data and the analytic capabilities in those specific areas, and the facilitation skills, to help people move improvement forward in all those areas." In short, he says, the job of the CCE is "to help facilitate improvement across the full spectrum, to understand the opportunity for data and analysis, facilitate improvement by working with nurses, physicians, and other leaders, to help them improve care and processes, and to monitor and track how we're doing, by creating an ongoing metric system."

It is in the comprehensiveness of creating that closed loop of observation and discussion, data and process analysis, improvement work, and further, ongoing observation, that the BWH structure around quality transformation is exceptional. In this context, it should not be surprising that the hospital has won a spate of recent national quality awards, among them:

- The 2006 National Quality Health Care Award from the Washington, D.C.-based National Committee for Quality Health Care (NCQHC)
- The 2007 UHC Quality and Accountability Top Performer award from the Oak Brook, Illinois-based University HealthSystem Consortium (UHC)
- Placement as one of the Washington, D.C.-based Leapfrog Group's list of 41 "Top Hospitals" for making significant strides in quality and patient safety
- Placement as one of the nation's top 100 hospitals and also a top performance improvement leader, by the Stamford, Connecticut-based Thomson Healthcare, in its 2007 "Thomson Top 100 Hospitals" list

In accepting the NCQHC award on behalf of BWH in 2006, Gary Gottlieb, MD, MBA, the organization's CEO, said simply, "There's always a sense here that we can do better. And we're willing to use science to figure it out. We had research showing that there were too many errors. Even one-tenth of one percent is a lot if you have millions of med administrations. That's thousands of people you could kill." Gottlieb's statement, which appeared in the NCQHC's report on the award, appeared in an article by the NCQHC that stated that "Brigham's culture of quality provides an example for hospitals nationwide."[2] Among the key factors the organization cited in bestowing its award on BWH:

- A culture of leadership, which encompasses the use of "a hospital-wide performance management called the Balanced Scorecard"
- "Brigham's clinical enterprise strategic plan, adopted in 2003, [which] includes developing five centers of excellence, in cancer, cardiovascular, women's health, neurosciences, and orthopedics, which account for more than 70% of inpatients, and adopting a 'distributed campus' strategy to provide the right care to the right patients in the right place, whether on the main campus or through remote ambulatory sites or partner facilities"
- The commitment of BWH's staff and clinicians to quality of care;
- The use of the Balanced Scorecard to help continuously improve care quality and patient satisfaction
- Strong and rigorous financial management

Robust Data Processes Critical

That the NCQHC's award recognized the use of the Balanced Scorecard approach and robust data analysis and analysis-driven improvement work was obviously no accident. Everywhere at BWH, there has been a very strong emphasis on the use of data tools and information to improve care quality and patient safety. That use encompasses both observation-based data analysis from within the organization, but also the use of clinical evidence from the medical literature to inform best practices and help shape the context for quality and safety improvement work itself.

CIO Sue Schade says she is heavily involved in working with quality leaders at the hospital to move things forward. "As the CIO, there are several things I do in terms of my position," she explains. "Number one, there is a board-level committee called the Care Improvement Council, it's Brigham-level, with clinical VPs, and our clinical chiefs are on it. And it is chaired by our chief medical officer. That group reviews all our quality, care improvement, process improvement, patient safety data activities in the organization, and it meets monthly. I'm part of that committee and never miss it. There's also a group called the Quality Outcomes Group.

Michael [Gustafson] runs that and it's co-chaired with our CMO and CNO. That group is composed of mid-level department-level folks involved with quality and safety initiatives. That group sets goals for the year and monitors progress. I participate actively in that. The person who reports to me, a physician, is the corporate manager for clinical information systems, and has the title IS director for clinical informatics."

And, Schade adds, she never misses her turn to participate in the Executive WalkRounds™. Not only does it send an important signal to everyone at BWH that IT is there to support and facilitate quality and patient safety improvement; it continually adds to her familiarity with processes—and people. "We're a 747-bed hospital," she underscores. "This is an academic medical center, with quaternary care, and it's huge. It's a teaching hospital, so the floors are busy with residents and interns, fellows, etc., so it's impossible for me to know every single clinician personally. But a lot of people do get to know me, as I show up regularly for these WalkRounds. I just feel it helps me to stay grounded. And I've added in the last few months bringing someone from my staff—one of my managers—with me."

Not many CIOs have such extensive day-to-day encounters with frontline clinicians. But then again, BWH is clearly not the average hospital. With regard to the organization's absolute commitment to quality transformation, "I think it's the most important thing we do. I'm involved in many areas, but I feel a special commitment to this, because it's the core of what we do."

As Gandhi and her co-authors pointed out in an August 2003 article in the *Joint Commission Journal on Quality and Safety*:

> Increasing reporting will be futile if robust systems are not in place to ensure that appropriate analysis and follow-up will take place. Before the Patient Safety Team was created, events were evaluated in line-item fashion, and physicians were not part of this evaluation process, which was conducted by nursing and pharmacy. The Patient Safety Team has created a database that includes all incident report data. Quarterly reports highlight trends by severity, time, and frequency. These reports, which are created for individual services, locations, and event types, are distributed to committees (for example, drug safety committee, falls committee) that are accountable for various types of incidents and to clinical nursing and medical leadership. The patient safety manager works with the various groups to evaluate observed trends and, when appropriate, with service-based multidisciplinary improvement

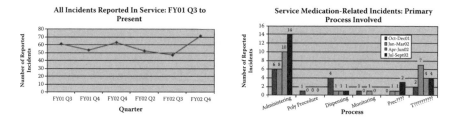

FIGURE 4.1.
Quarterly incident reports highlight trends by severity, time, and frequency. Two of the six reports—Incident Reports: Type of Incident and Injury, Incident Reports: Location of Incidents, Slip/Fall Incidents: Type of Fall, Service Medication-Related Incidents: Primary Process Involved and Injury, Blood Product-Related Incidents: Primary Process Involved and Injury, and Operating Room Incidents: Type of Incident—are shown.

teams to direct appropriate interventions. Tracking and trending data can help with both prioritization and identification of the underlying systems or process issues.

When reports are produced every quarter, they look (in part) like this (Figure 4.1).

Very importantly, of course, there is a cycle of event reporting, analysis, resolution, and feedback that is used to ensure that information is acted upon and used to further advance the entire push towards improved quality and patient safety. That cycle looks like this:

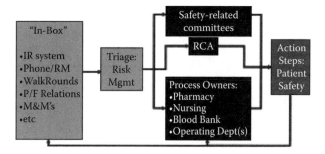

FIGURE 4.2.
This figure shows the flow of information through the current risk management and patient safety structure. IR, incident reporting; RM, risk management; P/F, patient/family; M & Ms, morbidity and mortality forums; RCA, root cause analysis.

It is this rigorous, data-driven approach that drives work forward at BWH, and ensures the objectivity and collaborative teamwork of the transformative quality work moving ahead at the hospital.

Can intensive, continuous work on quality and patient safety improvement be successful? The leaders at BWH have proven that it can be. Gandhi notes that "Establishing a reputation within an organization" can reap great rewards for quality and patient safety leaders, Gandhi says. "When we created the Patient Safety Team we wanted to establish a reputation for listening to feedback and following up. We wanted people to say things like, yes, if you want something to get done, call the Patient Safety Team."

And, adds Gustafson, achieving early wins is crucial. "That's true all the time, in fact, on several different levels. Executive leadership often wants to see outcomes and wins, so showing that you can accomplish those" is vital.

In the end, all those working on quality and patient safety transformation at BWH agree that intensive, strategically guided work will pay off, given sustained commitment and the shifting of an organization's culture towards one of learning and continuous progress forward. Executives at the majority of U.S. hospitals not as far along on the path would do well to heed such important lessons.

NOTES

1. Tejal K. Gandhi, MD, MPH, Erin Graydon-Baker, MS, RRT, Janet Nally Barnes, RN, J.D., Camilla Neppl, Carl Stapinski, R.Ph, Jon Silverman, Pharm.D, William Churchill, R.Ph, MS, Paula Johnson, MD, MPH, and Michael Gustafson, MD, MBA, "Creating an Integrated Patient Safety Team," *Joint Commission Journal on Quality and Safety*, Aug. 2003, Vol. 29, No. 8 (2003) 383.
2. NCQHC National Quality Health Care Award, 2006, special supplement: http://www.nqfexecutiveinstitute.org/qualityaward/ncqhc2006.pdf.

CASE STUDY 2

Seven San Francisco Bay Area Hospitals Pierce the Fog around Medication Administration Errors

Medication errors remain among the most common of medical errors in hospitals, and have been documented in an astonishingly wide range of studies and surveys in health care. One recent (July 2006) estimate from the Institute of Medicine found that medication errors harm at least 1.5 million people a year, and that the extra medical costs of treating drug-related injuries occurring in hospitals amount to $3.5 billion a year, a figure that does not take into account lost wages and productivity or additional health care costs.[1] An earlier estimate (2001) that appeared in the journal *Pharmacotherapy* found that medication errors occurred in 5.07% of the patients admitted every year to a group of 1,116 hospitals studied by a group of researchers led by C.A. Bond, PharmD[2] The *Pharmacotherapy* article authors further added that "Each hospital experienced a medication error every 22.7 hours (every 19.73 admissions). Medication errors that adversely affected patient care outcomes occurred in 0.25% of all patients admitted to these hospitals/year."

A number of pioneering hospitals have made inroads in this crucial area. Inevitably, the development of standardized processes around medication administration, and adherence to those standardized processes, is one element in overall medication management success stories.

One innovative grant-based program that ran for 18 months, concluding in March 2008, among seven San Francisco Bay area hospitals, and focused exclusively on the medication administration aspects of medication management, is offering important clues as to how medication administration can be optimized. The program, funded by a $5.8 million grant from the Gordon and Betty Moore Foundation (through its Betty Irene Moore Nursing Initiative) to the University of California, San Francisco's Center for the Health Professions, achieved strong outcomes among the seven participating hospitals (Kaiser Permanente-Fremont, Kaiser Permanente-Hayward, Novato Community Hospital, San Francisco General Hospital, St. Rose Hospital [Hayward], Stanford Hospital and Clinics [Palo Alto], Sequoia Hospital [Redwood City]).

The program was developed by the Integrated Nurse Leadership Program (INLP), one of the core research and professional development programs of the University of California, San Francisco's Center for the Health Professions. The INLP's 18-month program trained front-line clinicians, primarily nurses, to take a leadership role in developing clinical protocols, reporting tools and metrics, and administrative procedures, in the medication administration area.

INLP director Julie Kliger, MPA, BSN, the INLP's program director, reports that the participating hospitals, adhering to six process steps identified by the California Nursing Outcomes Coalition (CalNOC) as best practices for medication administration, improved medication administration accuracy from a baseline rate of 83.8% at the start of the program to 93.0% after 18 months. What's more, that 93.0% rate is based on documented, or "observed" accuracy, as the program made use of shadow observers who followed nurses as they administered medications to patients and then documented the results, rather than being based on self-reported accuracy rates.[3]

The six CalNOC best-practices process steps for medication administration to which program participants adhered were:

- The nurse is required to compare a medication to the medical record for the patient to whom the medication will be administered.
- The nurse must not be distracted or interrupted from the time the medication is taken in hand until it is administered to the patient.
- The medication must be labeled from the time it is taken in hand to the time it is delivered to the patient.
- The nurse must check two forms of identification on the patient; and, when appropriate, the nurse must explain the medication to the patient at the time of administration.
- The nurse must document the administration of the medication to the patient in the chart immediately after it is administered.

In addition, nurses were required to check for the classic "five rights" of medication administration: right patient, right time and frequency of administration, right dose, right route, right drug. As a result, medication administration errors dropped by 56.8% during the course of the program's 18 months. In addition, adherence to the six best practices, which started out at 79.5% at the outset of the program, increased to 91.8% at its conclusion. All these improvements took place across an average of 55 to 80 medication administrations per nurse per eight-hour shift at participating hospitals.

What accounts for the jump? "You have to employ front-line clinicians to solve front-line problems," Kliger says. "And, having worked as a nurse, I really think that it was very critically important to me to have a large component of professional efficacy taught throughout the program," she adds. Though she says she hesitates to use the oft-bandied-about term "nurse empowerment," she does believe that giving the nurses responsibility and authority to help design and implement changes, and to exert their authority as clinicians, was one of the keys to the success of the program, along with systemic thinking and process improvement.

For example, Kliger reports, in order to maintain strict adherence to the second of the six core best-practice process steps, around non-interruption of nurses during the medication administration process, participating hospitals instituted new procedures that Kliger herself had derived from the "sterile cockpit" concept in the aviation industry. The core concept, she says, comes from the idea that "From pushback to taking off the tarmac, you do not interrupt the pilot unless it's safety- or procedure-related. So," she says, "I translated that idea to the concept that from the moment the nurse walks into the meds room to obtain the medication, until adminis-tration to the patient at the bedside, the nurse should not be interrupted." As a result, participating hospitals instituted a new process in which, if a nurse were paged during the time that nurse was administering medica-tions, the nurse would allow the page to be answered by another party, sometimes a special "resource nurse" who was specifically assigned to that duty. Sometimes, the unit secretary or resource nurse was even given a detailed script to follow in responding to pages from doctors, the labora-tory, or family members, indicating essentially that the nurse was in the middle of a very important patient care process.

One of the underlying problems in this whole area, Kliger says, is that nurses end up shouldering so many of the responsibilities of the patient safety and quality mandates being imposed on hospitals externally by such organizations as the Joint Commission. Only when floor nurses are released from the web of constant distractions at critical moments can processes like medication administration be improved, she says.

Another underlying issue that the program exposed, Kliger says, was reflected in a study she recently read, in which researchers "went in and did something like an ethnography of nurses, and studied their flow and work patterns. They also identified different nurse characteristics; and one is that nurses deal with whatever the situation is, and accomplish the task at hand. So, the knowledge that nurses have that a process is broken, and the understanding of how to fix that process, never go anywhere." It is only through systems thinking and the application of performance improve-ment methodologies and formal strategies at a systemic level that many of the broken processes in hospitals are finally fixed, she says, since when processes contain problems that bedevil nurses' work, those problems are inevitably seen as trivial.

As a result, Kliger says, the INLP's training regimen for this program focused on skills development to support nurses' new role in the program, in the following areas: role identification, delegation, initiating change, conflict resolution, effective communication, dealing with informal authority, and lateral-level management.

In addition to the critical success factors of empowering and training nurses, applying systems thinking and concepts from other industries to the medication administration process, and strongly emphasizing adherence to consensus-driven best practices in this area, Kliger says there was one additional critical success factor. "Having an external driver like what we are as the sponsoring agent, where our priorities are always the program, was really important" to the success of the program, she says, "because of the fact that there are always competing priorities in hospitals, and everything always seems to trump quality and safety. But we're on the outside of those pressures, so we can be the external pressuring force that compels change."

One testimonial that she thinks speaks volumes about the value of initiatives such as the INLP's medication administration program came in March 2008, when the INLP held a recognition day for the clinicians involved in the program from the seven participating hospitals. "We held an event day to outline the results," she reports, "and had all the clinical teams there, along with executives from the participating hospitals. And one executive stood up and said, 'I've been a quality director in previous jobs for 15 years, and the nurse executive at my hospital for seven years, and without a doubt, this has been the most transformational experience I've ever had.' And that sentiment was not uncommon" that day, Kliger says. "Why? Because people were engaged; and they were fixing their own problems, and being recognized for doing so."

NOTES

1. "Medication Errors Injure 1.5 Million People and Cost Billions of Dollars Annually": National Academies press release, July 20, 2006. http://www8.nationalacademies.org/onpinews/newsitem.aspx?RecordID=11623. (accessed July 2008)
2. "Medication Errors in United States Hospitals." C.A. Bond, PharmD, FASHP, FCCP, Cynthia L. Raehl, PharmD, FASHP, FCCP, and Todd Franke, PhD, *Pharmacotherapy*. Pharmacotherapy 21, no. 9 (2001): 1023–1036. http://www.medscape.com/viewarticle/409777.

3. "USCF Program Achieves over 56% Reduction in Medication Administration Error": press release, March 26, 2008. http://www.reuters.com/article/pressRelease/idUS211440+26-Mar-2008+BW20080326 (accessed July 2008)

CASE STUDY 3

Children's Hospital of Wisconsin Exemplifies Pediatric Hospital Innovation

U.S. pediatric hospitals as a group are turning out to be among the most innovative types of hospitals when it comes to working to improve patient care quality and patient safety, and the core reason is obvious: The youngest patients in hospitals are among the most vulnerable to medical errors and sub-optimal care (along with, it could be argued, the frail elderly).

Indeed, "While the underlying quality and patient safety approaches are very similar no matter what setting patients are in, the stakes in pediatric hospitals are very high," observes Ramesh Sachdeva, MD, PhD, DBA, vice-president for quality and outcomes at the 236-bed Children's Hospital of Wisconsin (CHW), in Milwaukee. What's more, he adds, "We deal with children as patients, so the patient interactions are different. And unlike at the adult hospital where the main contact person is the patient himself, here, we're dealing with parents, so there's a strong need for family involvement. And even before the quality movement gained momentum, 10 years ago, we were including patients and families in our ICU rounds. And the structure of the children's hospital is different, it's more child-friendly."

Sachdeva agrees that the high stakes for patient outcomes are a strong motivating force for quality teams at pediatric hospitals to go the extra mile to improve patient safety and care quality. In the light of such reports as the study published in *Pediatrics: The Official Journal of the American Academy of Pediatrics*,[1] in which researchers found that 1 out of 15 children in children's hospitals are exposed to medication errors, Sachdeva says that medication and other medical errors are a high-priority target for pediatric hospital quality pioneers.

A Constellation of Efforts

At Children's Hospital of Wisconsin, Sachdeva says the organization went strategic with regard to quality and patient safety transformation several years ago. Indeed, one of the most concrete signals that the hospital was becoming more strategic in those areas came in 2002, when Sachdeva's position was created. Sachdeva meets every Tuesday with other senior executives, including the hospital's COO, CMO, CNO, vice-president of patient care services, vice-president of access and referral, and vice-president of ambulatory care, to do executive planning, budgeting, and analysis. "I'm integral to that group, especially on budgeting issues," he notes. "And that allows us to coordinate our strategies at the executive level in alignment with the insights of our front-line staff," who generate many ideas for improvement that later become projects and initiatives.

Numerous projects and initiatives have blossomed at Children's Hospital of Wisconsin, most involving core front-line clinical and administrative staff, and most also making use of Six Sigma, Lean management, or PDCA/PDSA (Plan, Do, Check, Act/Plan, Do, Study, Act) performance improvement methodologies.

One recent example has been a push to reduce the incidence of unlabeled or mislabeled specimens received in the lab. That project (whose team used Six Sigma data analysis strategies), which has resulted in a routine process that went live in the summer of 2007, gathered together a team of clinicians, including the lab manager, lab diagnostics QI/projects coordinator, a patient care manager, and one staff nurse from each of the three following units: the pediatric intensive care unit (PICU), the emergency department trauma center, and the hematology/oncology/transplant unit (it was those three units that had historically experienced the highest incidence of unlabeled or mislabeled lab specimens).

The team's goal, reports Ellen Flynn, RN, MBA, J.D., director of clinical transformation and patient safety at CHW, was to reduce to zero the incidence of unlabeled and mislabeled specimens sent from those three units, and to then spread the change in process to all of the hospital's patient care units. Among the obstacles the team encountered included limited time for team meetings and observation studies.

One key success factor, Flynn says, was the adoption of a protocol that nurses had mentioned had already vastly improved blood product identification and verification in a previous improvement project: The use of a short checklist identifying the essential steps for the clinicians verifying the right blood product for the right patient and administering a blood product.

To eliminate the incidence of mislabeled and unlabeled specimens, the clinician involved must now:

- Ensure that patients are wearing a correct ID band
- Fill out and initial each label
- Match each lab label to the patient ID band (two points of identification)
- Obtain the needed specimen and immediately label it in the presence of the patient

To promote adoption of the new process, unit supervisors handed out cards to staff they "caught" correctly labeling specimens, Flynn reports. The cards came with a piece of chocolate and a tear-off invitation that could be given to a peer inviting them to "catch the buzz." Since its inception in the spring of 2007, the process has been adopted in all inpatient care units.

Important lessons have been learned from the work done on the project, Flynn says. "We actually learned a really great lesson from the nurses on this team," she emphasizes. "It was because of the recommendation from the nurses working on the project that we tried using a checklist for the lab specimen verification process, since that had been a key element in our previous blood product verification project; and that suggestion worked." Using a checklist is "a process that's so basic, and is commonplace and routine in the aviation industry. By doing the data collection and using this check-off sheet, they became more compliant in that process." Not only was the adoption of a protocol common in another industry (as at other pioneer organizations, Children's Hospital of Wisconsin leaders have adopted ideas common to aviation in particular, in working to enhance patient safety) important in itself. How the adoption occurred, Flynn says, "showed us how important it was having front-line workers giving us feedback we wouldn't have understood ourselves. And it validated the use of evidenced-based processes, just as the aviation industry has used checklists in applying safety principles."

As at other pioneer quality and patient safety organizations, leaders at Children's Hospital of Wisconsin have endeavored to make the improvement process as strategic, broad, and objective as possible. "I've been here nine years," Sachdeva says, "and in that time, we've taken a very broad view of quality, a very organizational view of quality strategy. And a key success factor has been our approach of bringing the science of quality into practice. That's important, because frequently there's a pushback from physicians, who feel that quality really isn't an objective science. We need more scientific rigor. And that has resulted in some pushback from physicians."

Fortunately, he continues, "We have very strong data; and we have a full department collecting and analyzing data. But we've also tried to take it a notch higher, which means we've affirmatively tried to bring scientific approaches to match the methodology to the improvement challenge. Unlike many hospitals . . . We do Six Sigma, Lean management, and PDSA/PDCA, all three running concurrently." Rather than cling to methodology orthodoxy, "We check to see which methodology fits each problem," he says. He and his colleagues have also incorporated the use of health care operational research (OR) concepts in their work. These concepts are still used relatively rarely in health care, he concedes; but they were central to the development of a new model to optimize physician and nurse staffing in the pediatric intensive care unit (PICU) at CHW. He and his colleagues recently published an article about their work on that initiative in the *Journal of the Operational Research Society*.[2] In it, they describe the detailed data analysis that went into making an important management/operational decision on how to best use clinician resources in a key patient care unit.

Sachdeva, Flynn, and their colleagues have also benefited strongly from the involvement of Carl G. M. Weigle, MD, the hospital's medical director of information services and CMIO, and his team's strategic deployment of information technology to support the quality and patient safety transformation work at Children's Hospital of Wisconsin. Weigle notes that "We were the first pediatric facility in the country to go live with CPOE"—computerized physician order entry—when they flipped the switch in June 2000.

"One of the biggest lessons for us" in the realm of IT to support patient safety, Weigle says, "has been the recognition that CPOE implementation by itself is really just laying down a safety infrastructure. You can put alerts in and force people to follow certain procedures. But the major progress comes when you create an integration of the order entry system with pharmacy, or at least a two-way interface, and some automation of medication administration documentation such as barcoding or RFID [radio-frequency identification]—you have to tie those things all together in a loop, and we're working on that—that's where the big advances take place." Enterprise-wide barcoded medication administration went live between December 2006 and June 2007. And CPOE and clinical decision support have been used to help facilitate a number of important quality and safety initiatives since then, he notes.

Most of all, Sachdeva emphasizes, all the senior executives and clinician leaders at Children's Hospital of Wisconsin have worked very hard, together, to create a culture of learning, with rock-solid ongoing support from the CEO and executive management of the organization. "We're always working towards that learning culture," he says "we haven't completed it. But we have succeeded at creating a culture of continued learning, building on what we've learned previously. Second, we are indeed a very data-driven organization. And third, we've worked very hard to have a culture of openness and trust, so that people are willing to share their data. So if a physician's data is shared, that physician can have confidence that it's being shared for the right reasons." That has created crucial physician buy-in at CHW, he says. "We're also creating a culture of transparency," he concludes. "We're not completely transparent yet, but we're very close to it."

NOTES

1. Glenn S. Takata, Wilbert Mason, Carol Taketomo, Tina Logsdon, and Paul J. Sharek, "Development, Testing, and Findings of a Pediatric-Focused Trigger Tool to Identify Medication-Related Harm in US Children's Hospitals," *Pediatrics: Official Journal of the American Academy of Pediatrics* 121 (2008): e927–e935. Online at http://www.pediatrics.org/cgi/content/full/121/4/e927.
2. R. Sachdeva, T. Williams and J. Quigley, "Mixing methodologies to enhance the implementation of healthcare operational research," *Journal of the Operational Research Society,* September 2006. doi:10.1057/palgrave.jors.2602293.

5

Case Studies 4 to 6: Breakthroughs in Evidence-Driven Quality and in Clinical Decision Support for Improved Care

Geisinger Health System's ProvenCare program is unique in health care. The Pennsylvania health system's clinician leaders have, in a single program, created a protocols-based clinical quality optimization program that is also offering the first guaranteed pricing for selected surgical procedures in the industry. What's more, the story behind the story is even more compelling than the marquee headlines (pp. 64–70).

Bill Fera, MD, and his colleagues at the 20-hospital University of Pittsburgh Medical Center (UPMC) have been busy creating breakthroughs in areas where very few hospital organizations have ventured. Most interestingly, they have co-developed, with an IT vendor, a breakthrough system for interoperability that is giving UPMC physicians a unified view of patient care (pp. 71–74).

While some patient care organizations are taking very focused approaches to optimizing care quality and patient safety, others are pursuing a range of different strategies and efforts under a broad umbrella quality banner. At the 897-bed Northwestern Memorial Hospital in downtown Chicago, the approach has been to pursue a variety of efforts, all linked philosophically and conceptually, across a highly diverse range of clinical areas (pp. 74–80).

CASE STUDY 4

Geisinger Health System's Industry Breakthrough on Quality and Transparency

All of the case studies presented in this book share several common characteristics of pioneering patient care organizations: all involve strategic thinking; all involve organized action and sustained commitment to bring about change; all involve the strategic use of health care information technology to facilitate or empower innovation; and above all, every single case study in this book underscores the fundamental requirement of personal leadership by one individual or a small group of individuals to initiate and prompt transformative change in some area of care quality, patient safety, or workflow improvement.

None of these case studies exemplifies better the core requirement of personal leadership than does the transformation saga that has taken place at the three-hospital, 41-clinic, integrated Geisinger Health System. Geisinger Health System provides care to 2.5 million people in 41 counties across northeastern and central Pennsylvania from its base in the town of Danville, which is located about one hour north of the state's capital of Harrisburg. As described in *Paradox and Imperatives in Health Care,* Geisinger took an unprecedented step in February 2006, when it launched its revolutionary ProvenCare program, in which, for the first time in the health care industry, a hospital-based organization set a guaranteed, publicly announced price guarantee on a major surgical procedure (coronary artery bypass graft, or CABG), and tied that transparent pricing initiative to its own internally developed quality optimization program.

Since the establishment of the CABG element of the ProvenCare program, Geisinger leaders have extended the concept out to encompass an ever-widening circle of clinical procedures, including total hip replacement surgery and cataract surgery.

But beyond the expanding scope of the program, what is most noteworthy of all this work is the role that executive and clinician leadership has played in its evolution. Fundamentally, ProvenCare came about because of the leadership of a new clinician CEO and the personal championship of a physician leader.

The story begins in March 2001, when Glenn Steele, Jr., MD, PhD, became the new president and CEO of the Geisinger Health System, after decades of practice as a surgeon and years of experience in academic leadership at the University of Chicago. The opportunity to initiate some kind of transformative clinical quality improvement was in fact "one of the two primary reasons why I came here several years ago," Steele says. "Having spent 24 years in various academic environments, of which almost 20 years was leadership, I was convinced that the generation of new clinical knowledge, as good as it had been for me in Boston and Chicago, was rate-limiting in helping human beings. So one of the two reasons for coming to Geisinger from a wonderful institution, the University of Chicago, was to be a part of a very unusual culture, to see if we could be transformative. And the other reason was to see whether I could do a turnaround."

Steele's core objective was very simple, at least conceptually: He wanted to prove that clinical quality transformation was possible and doable in an inpatient setting. And he saw the Geisinger organization as ripe for mission-driven change. "I saw an organization here that had great governance and had a wonderful financial and HR balance sheet, but that had become immersed in a dysfunctional merger" with the Penn State-Hershey system, he says. "I was the first CEO to join at a time when the organization was just coming out of that dysfunctional merger. So I was able to bring people together to coalesce under a single, unified vision. And that was really fun."

Of course, it has required a lot of work, too. But the key first step took place shortly after his arrival, when Steele put forward the goal of clinical transformation as one of the organization's key strategic goals. Soon, he was meeting with various groups of specialist physicians, promoting the idea, and soliciting physician champions to take up the cause. Fortunately, he found Alfred Casale, MD, surgical director at the Geisinger Heart Institute, which oversees surgical work across three facilities, and is located in the organization's flagship hospital, Geisinger Medical Center, in Danville.

As Dr. Casale recalls it, "We had just put together the cardiac surgery unit as a service line, and I had only been here a year, when Glenn asked me to spearhead the inclusion of surgery within cardiac services. And part of my goal within that was to reduce the degree of unnecessary idiosyncrasy within the platforms" among the organization's cardiac surgeons, whose corps was quickly growing. "What I found when I first got here was a very high level of skill, with excellent outcomes," Casale says, "but the concept that was defended at all costs was individual physician prerogative, a fairly traditional concept." As a result, he notes, there were three surgeons specializing in deep-vein thrombosis, and four pathways just for the prevention of deep-vein thrombosis, for example. One of those pathways had not yet been eliminated, though it had been created by a surgeon who had left two years previously. As a result, he says, "The first question physician assistants would ask the nurse about any particular atrial fibrillation was, whose patient is he? Because who the attending was would dictate the next step of managing the situation. And that's nuts!"

As a result, Casale was determined to introduce greater clinical practice standardization across the ten surgeons and three hospitals, in order to eliminate unnecessary variation and improve patient safety. And, he says, "We were about a year into that work, when Glenn threw down the gauntlet on quality," asking for physician leaders to volunteer to help create clinical transformation. Casale volunteered himself and the CABG area as a laboratory for change, determining that CABG was a good clinical area to focus on, since it involved a small number of specialist physicians already working at a high skill level; already had strong clinical outcomes; had a broad and deep clinical literature on which to rely for evidence; and involved a complex enough process with a variety of sub-elements that was meaty enough to be interesting for clinicians to take on. What's more, the American College of Cardiology and American Heart Association had just publicly adopted revised deadlines for coronary grafting. "The problem with those guidelines, however, is that they're quite generic," Casale notes. "They include things like, 'use antibiotics appropriately.'"

So, Casale organized all of his surgeon colleagues who performed CABG operations and divided up the work of translating the broad guidelines from the clinical literature into 41 discrete procedural steps that would provide measurement and benchmark foundations for the program. At the same time, finance department managers at Geisinger got busy charting out a path toward the groundbreaking innovation of offering a guaranteed price point (between $25,000 and $30,000 per surgery in 2007) for elective CABG patients.

Back on the clinical side, Casale says that several core principles guided their intensive work. Chief among these were:

- Avoid unnecessary idiosyncrasy. This was critical.
- Using authoritative, evidence-based guidelines and information from the clinical literature was a foundation for building every procedural step.
- Rigorous analysis of evidence from the literature and consensus-driven translation of that evidence into the procedural steps was core to the group's approach.
- Designing the procedural steps, or pathways, was done with the goal of maximizing the flexibility and interchangeability of clinical work across the various participating hospitals: in other words, helping the surgeons, as well as the nurses and other assistive clinicians, to streamline and standardize surgical processes across the system was a goal, so that surgeons could more easily substitute for one another at the system's different hospitals, as needed.
- Having every cardiac surgeon involved in the design process ensured clinical consensus and, later on, compliance.

One absolutely critical success factor was the decision to allow for surgeon opt-outs with regard to any of the 41 steps in the consensus-built CABG pathway. Any surgeon who wishes to opt out of any of the 41 steps in the pathway may do so; but that doctor must document in the organization's electronic medical record the reasons for doing so, and all opt-outs are retrospectively reviewed by the group as a whole. Interestingly, from the time that the CABG program went live, in February 2006, through February 2008 (when he was interviewed for this book), only five opt-outs were taken; and that is five opt-outs from individual steps in the 41-step protocol, and across 200 surgeries. In other words, a little over one-twentieth of one percent of all possible opt-outs were taken, indicating an extraordinary rate of protocol compliance.

In any transformative work, "Getting clinician buy-in is a difficult challenge," says Ronald A. Paulus, MD, MBA, Geisinger's chief technology and innovation officer, "but it's one with great rewards. To get that buy-in, an organization's leaders must articulate and live a vision that provides a guiding principle, that focuses on what's right for the patient," he says. What's more, he adds, "Over time, the process built steam, and we took away some of the fears, like 'cookbook medicine.' We said, we're not going to force anybody to do anything they don't think is clinically right. But we're going to look at the literature, and if you want to go against something in the literature, you're going to have to document why not." Fortunately, he adds, "Physicians and clinicians are data-driven, and respond to the evidence, if they think it's good."

As a result of this initial success, Geisinger's experience with the CABG program has not only spurred further ProvenCare development—in areas that now include hip replacement and cataract surgery (both of which are in various states of pilot or go-live development); it has helped spur further quality transformation in general at the system. When asked about the key success factor of achieving physician buy-in for the ProvenCare CABG program, Casale says that "Three things created buy-in. One was that it was supported so strongly by the board and the executive management team. Two, it was respectfully done by people helping to design the translation, and specifically, the ability to address the ones they were most skeptical of. And three, we created this ability to use an opt-out option to personalize your patients' needs. And what people recognized very quickly was that by removing all these 40 elements that I had to take care of from my personal consciousness and putting it into, in a sense, the institutional unconscious, people were so much more sanguine that patients would get the right stuff."

What's more, Casale says, "There's nothing about the 40 elements that's magic, absolutely nothing. Any good cardiac surgeon does most of these most of the time; the problem is that nobody, unless they're at Geisinger, would bet the fact that any individual patient got all of them. I would bet my retirement that the guy I did today, got all 40 elements. But the ability to redesign a system, to guarantee a process, that's magic."

The results have been gratifying to all involved. Within the first year of the CABG program, the CABG mortality rate had dropped from 1.5% to 0%; pulmonary complications had dropped from 7.3% to 2.6%; readmission within 30 days had dropped from 6.6% to 5.1%; and average length of stay had decreased 16%.

TEACHING THE CULTURE OF QUALITY

At press time, there were numerous clinical transformation initiatives taking place at Geisinger; the success of the CABG program under the ProvenCare umbrella is only the most spectacular and visible example of the work taking place system-wide. What can fairly be said with regard to Geisinger overall is that CEO leadership, abetted by stand-up clinician leadership, has led to a system-wide commitment to transformative quality and process change.

Karen McKinley, RN, MBA, vice-president in the Division of Clinical Effectiveness at Geisinger Health System, says that broad leadership from the top of the organization has helped to build a cultural focus on care quality improvement over time. "Dr. Steele challenged us a number of years ago to develop an education program, which we've dubbed Geisinger Quality Institute, which is in its third year," she says. "And I can say that a fair number of our front-line staff can speak that language [of transformative quality] competently. But it's a transition that takes years. We teach front-line interdisciplinary teams" the building blocks of quality work, McKinley says. And as of press time, 86 teams of five to six people per team on average (both clinicians and non-clinicians) had been trained in the tools and language of quality work. What's more, each team does a specific project as part of its training, producing a poster presentation based on a 90-to-120 day cycle of improvement, she adds.

Speaking of this team development, McKinley continues, "We've also tried to tie their work—micro-systems, we call it—to the broader quality issues and goals of the organization. How did they tie into the Institute of Medicine's Six Aims? How did they tie into our organizational goals?" Meanwhile, she says, "At the leadership level, we teach at a different level, explaining things conceptually, as well as tying them into things like literature reviews. And we're having the teams that complete their cycles present to the leadership groups." All of the organization's executives and middle managers have attended at least one session in which interdisciplinary teams have presented poster sessions based on projects, she notes.

The core philosophy behind this approach, McKinley says, is that "We want to teach people how they can improve their work, and not do it for them. We want to provide the facilitation and knowledge and tools, because improvement should happen every day."

One CEO's Perspective

CEO Steele acknowledges that Geisinger had some advantages going into its intensive quality transformation. For one thing, the system was doing relatively well in terms of productivity to begin with. "We're blessed here, because of our good operations and organization, in that people aren't working 16 hours a day scratching out an attempt to increase RUV requirements;

so we're able to tackle things other well-meaning people can't see to do," he says. "But," he quickly adds, "I think that every healthy, robust, institution has a moral obligation to do something as a part of their portfolio that is innovative and different."

As to where to begin transformative quality work, Steele says that "You start with what is under your control, and what can't hurt patients, that's the first thing. And if it's benefiting patients, and you can document it in some way," those characteristics also provide some guidance.

More broadly, he says, the work that began (and is continuing) with ProvenCare and that is also being pursued through a variety of different avenues across Geisinger (such as via the multidisciplinary team training work), should be understood in a bigger-picture context, as part of an overall drive towards a combination of optimized clinical quality, an improved cost and service profile, and far greater transparency in terms of both quality and cost, for purchasers, payers, and consumers.

"I think it will be a huge benefit if we can maintain quality and really cut down cost," Steele says. "And that's where we're going now. We're trying to link the metrics not only on quality but also on cost and service, across an entire case of care. And we need to market that in a transparent way and have the brokers—the health plans—or the business purchasers, choose based on value. That's the work of a lifetime," he concedes. But he adds that "My goal is to demonstrate through ProvenCare that we can actually demonstrate improved quality linked to lower costs for specific populations of patients."

Reinforcing the notion that attracting physician champions to the hard spade work of building programs like ProvenCare, Steele says that "One of the interesting aspects of this is that if you can find a key, credible clinician like an Al Casale, you can start in an area where there is evidence from the clinical literature. And once you get started and can actually show just a little bit of success—that's always been one of my keys of leadership—you get an affirmation circuit going. And then other people see it. And we've done this with Al, and now it's spread across the organization."

In the end, Steele says, both as a physician and as a senior executive, "What drives this is pride of purpose, and the affirmation from our clinical leaders knowing they're doing something that's important and can create change. Some of our best docs and nurses are a bit misanthropic, that's just the way they are. But if you can just find those early champions and show folks that it can work, people will be convinced."

Such has been the positive attention that has come Geisinger's way because of the success of ProvenCare for CABG and because of the organization's overall commitment to quality, that the health system's leaders are considering the possibility of packaging their approach and offering it to other hospitals and health systems in some form. As Steele says, "We're looking at the possibility of partnering with national organizations to bring this out nationally, because there's only so much that can be done by a single organization." From his perspective, the work that Geisinger is doing in terms of quality, cost-effectiveness, and transparency is absolutely a part of the broader national awakening to the potential of transformation. "I'm a pretty optimistic person naturally anyway," he says of the quality movement in health care. "But beyond that, I think we are realizing as a society is that we're not necessarily providing the best value" in patient care organizations. And there are enough people talking about it that it's making an impact. We've got terrific hospitals, clinicians and staff, and technology, but all of that is not good enough. We really have got to do better."

CASE STUDY 5

Groundbreaking Interoperability Gives UPMC Physicians a Unified View of the Patient Record

Bill Fera, MD, and his colleagues at the 20-hospital University of Pittsburgh Medical Center (UPMC) have been busy creating breakthroughs in areas where very few hospital organizations have ventured. Most interestingly, they have been pioneering in an often-overlooked, yet critical, area of clinical computing, and that is with regard to interoperability tools to support physicians at the point of care.

As any physician who has been frustrated at the lack of completeness of clinical information at the bedside can attest, most information systems remain woefully unconnected to one another, particularly across the inpatient-outpatient divide, as well as across all the disparate systems in a large multi-hospital organization like that of UPMC. Fera, a family physician by clinical specialty, is vice-president of medical technologies at UPMC.

As part of UPMC's strategy to implement an electronic medical record (EMR) across all the inpatient and outpatient settings in their vast organization, they created a partnership with an IT vendor that has created a leap forward in providing doctors with a comprehensive view of patient information from many disparate systems, all pulled neatly together onto a unified screen, and using an underlying common medical vocabulary that boosts geometrically the intelligence of the overall system.

In a nutshell, when a physician using this system (which went live in February 2008 at two hospitals in the UPMC system and is gradually being adopted by doctors across the organization) pulls up a particular patient's information, that doctor is able to see all the patient's data, from any of the disparate inpatient and outpatient software programs running across the organization (the main ones among them being the inpatient EMR, from the Kansas City, Missouri-based Cerner Corporation, and the outpatient EMR, from the Madison, Wisconsin-based Epic Systems Corporation), on a single screen, through a viewer tool, in a mostly tabular format. That in itself is something very few developers have been able to achieve.

But the bonus is that underlying work done by clinical and IT professionals at UPMC, as assisted by their vendor partner, within one month created a foundational medical vocabulary database, so that if a physician wants to determine whether the patient being cared for has been on any kind of penicillin-like drug, for example, all penicillin-like drugs recorded in any information system within the organization will appear on the screen at once. Laboratory and radiology data are also accessible, in text-based and graphical formats.

In order to achieve this breakthrough, Fera and his colleagues worked with experts at the Hod HaSharon, Israel-based dbMotion software firm. Physicians at some hospitals in Israel had already been working in such a unified-field environment, but virtually no hospitals in the United States had achieved the same kind of clinical environment in the same way. The term that the UPMC and dbMotion folks are using for the specialty capability of this program to draw together sought information from disparate systems through data systems as presented in unified fields is *semantic interoperability,* a term that a few other organizations are using as well, but that is being applied to this particular function in a unique way at UPMC. As dbMotion executives explain it, they had already developed a clinical vocabulary domain that was a part of the company's unified medical schema, and which was then further refined and reiterated in their co-development work with Fera and his colleagues at UPMC. Fortunately, Fera notes, as a medical IT leader, he had the advance of being able to work with a physician with exceptional expertise in medical vocabulary work, Dr. Bill Hogan, who spent about one month working with a pharmacist and a medical analyst to lay the vocabulary foundation that underlies the medication search capability at UPMC.

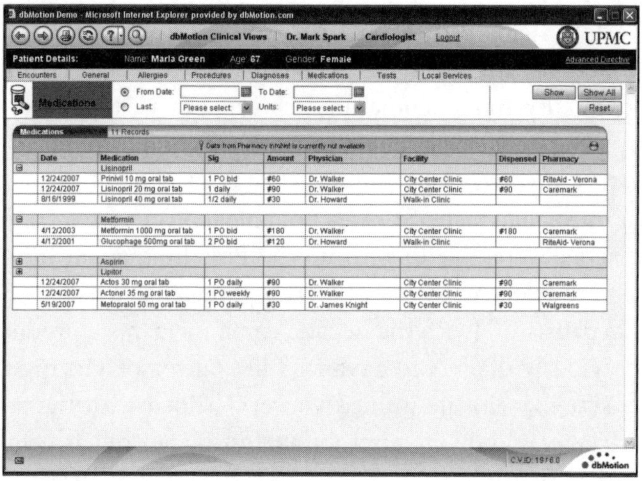

FIGURE 5.1. SAMPLE SCREEN.

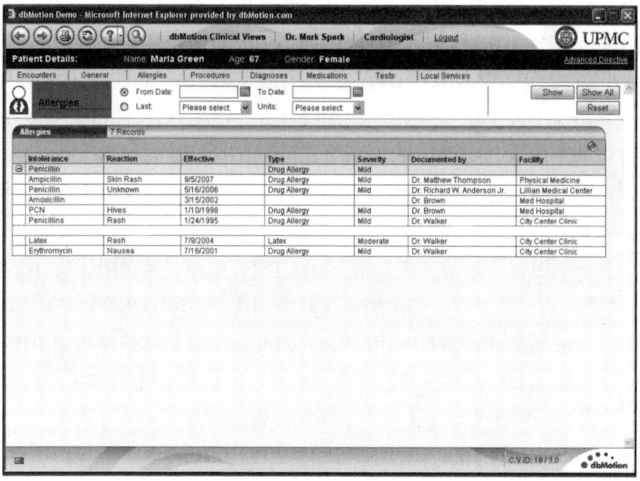

FIGURE 5.2. SAMPLE SCREEN.

In order to make all this more concrete, Fera provides a "for-instance" example. "Let's say I'm working in the emergency room," he begins. "And I'm seeing a patient who I think has pneumonia, and I'm going to prescribe an antibiotic. And I want to make sure that that patient is neither on any medications that the antibiotic would interfere with, such as Coumadin; nor on any medications which would interfere with the antibiotic. I also need to check for allergies. The historic challenge," he points out, "is that 85% of all patient information is not in the inpatient EMR. It's in the ambulatory systems. But with the dbMotion platform, I can go anywhere in the UPMC system, and through its viewer bring the information to myself, on a single, unified screen." Clearly, the potential for improving patient care quality and outcomes in such situations is tremendous.

Not surprisingly, lives can be saved. Fera says that "The most dramatic recent instance involved a patient who came into one of our emergency rooms in a somnolent state. She was not able to give us any information. And because we were able to get into the Epic [outpatient information] system, we were able to determine that this patient had a history of hepatic coma and hepatitis C" (with the hepatic coma incidents a product of that patient's previously diagnosed advanced liver disease). Having the comprehensive system, with its unified viewer, "helped with the streamlining of the diagnosis and with appropriate testing, as well as helping us to use appropriate precautions, per her hep C," Fera adds. Essentially, that patient's bloodstream had extremely toxic levels of ammonia that could not be cleared by her liver. "So it was a life-saving situation" to be able to use the advanced information system in this case and to be able to render the appropriate care quickly, he notes.

Will physicians gravitate towards using such systems? Absolutely, says Joel Diamond, MD, dbMotion's chief medical officer, North America. "Our experience in Israel and at UPMC is that this is viral: when the doctors hear about this, they're really, really thirsty to get more of it."

Indeed, Fera and his colleagues plan to continue to expand the availability and capabilities of this system for interoperability, in order to improve core patient care quality, assist in better organization disease management for patients with chronic illnesses, and better analyze patient care data and use it to help the organization thrive in pay-for-performance programs with payers.

"The biggest lesson to me," Fera says, "is that people tend to think of interoperability as a luxury or as an esoteric tool, whereas we've proven that it's an indispensable quality tool. And patients won't get the best care possible unless you offer a tool like this one. And through the quality measures and outcomes that you're going to get, you'll get the return on investment, but people really need to invest in these now," he urges. "People talk about patient-centered care; this is really patient-centered care."

CASE STUDY 6

Northwestern Memorial Hospital Clinicians Tackle an Array of Quality Challenges

Every hospital organization that is pursuing quality transformation is taking it on in a different way. Some organizations have very focused approaches, while others are pursuing a range of different strategies and efforts under a broad umbrella quality banner. An example of the latter type of organization is the 897-bed Northwestern Memorial Hospital, a prestigious academic medical center located in downtown Chicago. The Northwestern approach has been to pursue a variety of efforts, all linked philosophically and conceptually, across a highly diverse range of clinical areas.

The path towards quality transformation was, is, and remains a long and winding road, and a never-ending one inside hospital organizations committed to the cause, says Cynthia Barnard, director, quality strategies, at Northwestern Memorial. "The biggest challenge we know with quality improvement is sustaining change," says Barnard, who has spent nearly three decades working in the areas of quality improvement, patient safety, medical staff affairs, and clinical research. "That's what process improvement has done for us." In that regard, Barnard says, "We've created all-new resources in order to fully pursue process improvement here. That demonstrates the commitment of senior management and the board to putting our money where our collective mouth is, and to investing in the belief that such work will pay off in terms of improved quality."

With regard to the variety of efforts being pursued at Northwestern Memorial, Barnard reports that "We started out pursuing five or six projects a year; now we're up to 20 to 30 projects a year, with the cycle-time goal of completing projects within eight months," an aim she notes is ambitious, considering the scope of many of the projects. "The earlier projects tended to be directed at simple things like queuing and wait times," she reports. "Now they're more complex."

A few key elements in all this work, Barnard says, include the fact that there is a quality committee at the board of directors level, to begin with. Also, that that committee "has dramatically changed its focus and operations, so that now they're very much driven by a quality dashboard." Board members, she adds, "hold the management team to a pretty high standard to both rigor and ambition of goals. And board members are not only business and community leaders, but also patients and family members."

As at other organizations whose leaders are committed to quality transformation, the use of data in measurement, analysis, and feedback to stimulate further quality improvement work has been assuming an ever-larger profile at Northwestern Memorial. "Over the last five or six years, we've gone from what I would characterize as fairly timid use of measurement, to fairly bold measurement," Barnard says evenly. "You can't get ahead of your board, but you can't get behind them, either," she reflects. "The further you go along, the more you're asking your board to hold you to high standards. In terms of improvement, we were also looking at one particular measure, and the question was, is a 20% improvement a big improvement? So, we came up with the idea that for our very big goals, in general, our objective is to reach optimal performance, which usually means 95 to 100% of perfect, whatever that might mean for that goal, within two years. Within the first year, we wanted to be able to cover one-third of the gap between wherever we are and perfect, and then in the second year, close the gap. Let's say you're at 40% of universal hand hygiene adoption: you'll want to go from 40 to 60% the first year, and get to 100% the second year." The hospital's board, as it has become more educated about and engaged in the organization's efforts at quality transformation, has become highly supportive of moving forward aggressively, she says, to the point that "This last year, we launched a three-year plan with some very bold long-range goals. And we couldn't have done that a few years ago, because the board was not there yet."

Intelligently Implementing Smart Pumps

Among the numerous examples of transformational quality work at Northwestern Memorial has been the implementation in the past two years of so-called "smart" infusion pumps—intravenous infusion pumps that have microchips built into them and can be programmed to set use and dosage parameters and emit warnings when those parameters are exceeded. Numerous studies have found that the proper use of smart pumps can dramatically reduce medication errors involving IV pumps.

For example, Angela T. Cassano, PharmD, reported in a recent issue of *Hospital Pharmacy*[1] that when one five-facility community hospital system in Pennsylvania implemented smart infusion pumps, the system captured overrides and alerts in 2.6% of cases, while within four months, there were 10 "critical catches"—situations in which actual harm to a patient was averted by the system. In other words, a small but significant percentage of potential errors, including a smaller subset of potentially devastating errors, can clearly be averted through the intelligent implementation of a smart pump system.

Carol Payson, RN, M.S.N., director of surgical patient care, and Karen Cabansag, RN, manager of surgical patient care, have been among the leaders of the smart infusion pump implementation at Northwestern Memorial. The hospital went live with the new smart pumps in May 2007. Among the goals: to obtain real-time utilization data for quality improvement use, and to build a drug library, to facilitate the keying in of needed IV medications by nurses on the floors. Fundamentally, Payson says, "It was all about delivering safer patient care."

Indeed, says Cabansag, the traditional way of preparing infused medication is no longer acceptable in organizations working to transform their care quality. "What we were doing prior to the smart pumps is that we would look at the medication that came from pharmacy," Cabansag says. "We would enter the rate and the volume to be infused in the bag, for example, 1000 cc's. It wasn't specific to that medication." And that process was riddled with potential errors and missteps, above all, key-in errors.

As a result, clinicians at Northwestern Memorial, supported by the information systems team, went ahead and evaluated vendors, ultimately choosing one of two well-known vendors that had reached the finalist stage. Once the vendor was selected, Northwestern Memorial pharmacists developed a core template for that product, which was customized by the nurses and nurse managers to meet the needs of specific units at the hospital. Standardization was achieved in general, and then within each of the specialties (ICU, med-surg, etc.).

Nurses on the units practiced with the smart pumps before the actual go-live, working out issues with dosages, and, in a number of cases, customizing pumps on specific units where a special tubing or filter was needed, Cabansag reports. Post-implementation, a smart pump now beeps an alert if a nurse keys in an incorrect or improper drip rate or dosage.

Importantly, says Payson, "We worried that the nurses might find workarounds, but they didn't. They are being extremely compliant. We're thrilled," she adds.

And though the hospital did not keep organized data specifically on adverse IV medication errors prior to the rollout of the new smart pumps (what data did exist was part of the general database on adverse events), "Now, we've got data on all the pumps," Payson reports, "and we share that data with nursing. And we're finding that the alerts have helped avert errors," the most common of which had involved nurses inadvertently keying in the wrong drip rate on the old "dumb" pumps.

Interestingly, Payson says, "We've heard from very seasoned nurses who never thought they could make an error, who have reported that they've had alerts come up for them."

Barnard notes that "While pump errors are relatively frequent, most don't cause a lot of harm overall; but a small number of cases do cause a lot of harm." And it is those adverse events above all that clinicians at Northwestern Memorial are determined to prevent. Two additional steps that will enhance the installation of the smart pumps, she notes, are, first, the implementation of the use of barcoding for bedside medication administration, expected to go live sometime in 2009; and the integration of the smart pump parameters with the hospital's computerized physician order entry (CPOE) system also expected to be facilitated in the near future.

How does the implementation of "smart" infusion pumps fit into the push to create a culture of patient safety at Northwestern Memorial Hospital? "Anytime you can put alerts in place, put systems in place that help the caregiver do the right thing, it's very positive," Payson concludes.

Medication Reconciliation: Study Results and Culture Change

Gary Noskin, MD, Northwestern Memorial's associate chief medical officer, has been involved in medication reconciliation work on two broad fronts. Not only has he participated in the long-term efforts to help universalize the inpatient medication reconciliation process, in which a patient's medication history is recorded and documented, and in which discrepancies and problems are worked out during the patient's stay; he has also led the largest hospital-based scientific study of medication reconciliation issues to date, funded by the federal Agency for Healthcare Research and Quality (AHRQ). Not only have he and his team of researchers been able to uncover the biggest challenges to optimizing the management of medication information for inpatients; they have also used the conducting of the study to help change the culture around medication reconciliation among clinicians at Northwestern.

What did Noskin and his colleagues learn in conducting their study? As it turns out, Noskin reports, the most difficult part of creating an effective medication reconciliation process is obtaining an accurate and complete medication history and list to begin with. He notes that patients obtain their medications from a wide range of sources—from their primary care physicians, from their local pharmacies, from mail-order pharmacies, and so on. And even the taking of vitamins (which often contain calcium, which interacts with many medications) and herbal supplements, can play a role in medication effectiveness. What's more, they may be taking a variety of over-the-counter medications as well as prescribed drugs. Furthermore, if they are admitted to the hospital via the emergency department, they may not have been conscious or able to speak coherently at the time of admission. For all these reasons and a host of others, obtaining an accurate, complete medication history, which is the basis of a good medication reconciliation process, also turned out to be the single greatest challenge in that process, Noskin and his colleagues discovered, as they conducted their study in 2006 to 2007 (at press time, they were in the midst of analyzing the data from the study).

Among the key overall findings: first, that a broad majority of patient cases involve medication reconciliation discrepancies, which is significant; and that in order to perform effective medication reconciliation, a patient's medications have to be reconciled at least twice, once near the outset of the inpatient stay, and again prior to discharge. Noskin and his colleagues included data from all Northwestern Memorial patients; the number of patients whose cases were actively researched ran in the 700 to 800 range, he reports.

Given the fact that the overwhelming majority of patients entering any hospital as inpatients are on at least one prescription medication, and that most are on two or more, Noskin agrees that it is highly problematic that the state of medication reconciliation across the industry is still relatively primitive. But that is the case, he says, "Because this is really hard. We had a pharmacist who was expert in obtaining medication histories, do so as part of our study, and the average time it took for that clinician to obtain a medication history was 9.8 minutes, and that was time-consuming. Given that in private practice, most physicians have about 15 minutes of actual time with patients during the average patient visit, that becomes a nearly insurmountable barrier to effective medication reconciliation at the physician office level, he notes. In addition, he says, one of the other main learnings from the study has been the idea that medication reconciliation in the hospital setting is a process, not a single (or even double) event."

Though at press time, Noskin and his colleagues were sifting through the data from their study and working up their broad analysis, he says the conducting of the study has definitely enhanced medication reconciliation awareness and cooperation at Northwestern Memorial. All it takes is for physicians, nurses, and pharmacists to hear one or two anecdotes in order to change their attitudes and behaviors on the importance of doing medication reconciliation and getting it right.

In addition, Noskin says, an important learning for any organization that might attempt to move its medication reconciliation process forward is that "It's important to involve clinicians early on" in the work of moving medication reconciliation forward. How can hospitals make medication reconcilication successful? "The single most important factor is making the right thing to do be the easy thing to do as well," he says, "because anytime that you to ask clinicians to do things that will take more time, they'll do workarounds—and people in health care are quite adept at workarounds."

Organ Transplant ID Management: Self-Imposed Urgency

Often, a patient care organization moves forward in a particular area of quality transformation because of a sentinel event that has recently occurred within that organization; but not always. With regard to organ identification for transplantation, clinicians at Northwestern Memorial moved ahead to optimize their process following a famous sentinel event that occurred at another hospital organization in February 2003, when a 17-year-old female patient died, after a hospital internationally respected for its organ work had transplanted a heart and lung mismatched to the patient's blood type into her body, and she died following surgery. The case garnered national and international headlines, and caused clinicians leading Northwestern Memorial's organ transplant program to pause to consider whether such an incident could occur at Northwestern Memorial. Though no such incident had ever occurred at Northwestern, transplant program leaders agreed that it could possibly happen there at some point in the future.

As Michael Abecassis, MD, put it, "We asked ourselves, could this happen here? And it was clear that sometimes, if we had a couple of organs, especially kidneys, and they were sitting in pre-op boxes on ice, a mix-up could happen here"—with kidney transplant operations the most vulnerable to misidentification error, since kidneys are organs usually removed from a donor corpse elsewhere and then shipped to Northwestern Memorial. Abecassis, the chief of the Division of Organ Transplant, at Northwestern Memorial, and dean for clinical affairs at the Northwestern Medical School, and J. Roscoe Miller, Distinguished Professor in Surgery, Microbiology, and Immunology, says that at Northwestern Memorial, as at most patient care organizations, far too many processes continue to rely on the skills, expertise, and alertness of individual clinicians and staffers rather than on systems that can guard against harm and mishaps.

Abecassis also turned to an idea already in use in a different context, for a solution to the challenge of correctly identifying donated organizations 100% of the time. "We felt that we needed to have a system that was basically idiot-proof, that would let us be reassured as much as possible," he says. "But I said, why should we reinvent the wheel here? We go through a careful matching process with every unit of blood that comes in. So we went to talk to the director of our blood bank. He thought that applying that identification process to organ donations made sense. After all, when we receive blood donations either for organ transplant or in general, the blood type of the recipient is already entered into the computer every time." So essentially, Abecassis and his colleagues in the organ transplant division decided to piggyback on a system already in use with regard to one aspect of organ transplant, the blood donation/identification process.

As a result, an added system was established for organ identification, grafted onto the existing blood donation identification system, and managed by the organ transplant team managers. The system was established in 2004. Now, any organization (including Northwestern Memorial itself) that is releasing an organ does so using a process of multiple-checkpoint identification, following the same pattern used for identifying and processing units of blood, one that includes the use of identifying stickers, and the double-checking of the organ at every step of the transfer process. "For cadaver-provided organs," Abecassis specifies that "we give them the paperwork from the hospital from whence it came. And they check it and give a number, just as they do with a blood unit. And they send that form, and that's checked by two people, to make sure that that organ belongs to that patient, just as with a unit of blood."

No incident has occurred since that time, and, says Abecassis, he and his colleagues are feeling much more secure in their processes knowing that a system is in place to ensure organ ID verification. In the end, he says, the lesson learned here is that "There are two principles involved. First, the simpler you make it, the less likely you are to have an error. And when I start to think about fail-safe systems, if you start to come up with complicated algorithms, someone's going to get mixed up. And the second principle is to make a process familiar. We all know how the blood bank process works. That process is already in place and has stood the test of time, and people are already familiar with it, so rather than inventing some complicated new process, why not make it consistent with something that happens countless times a day? And it's very easy, it's a visual check of this against that, and if it doesn't match, then that raises an alert." For the time-pressed clinicians and staff who work in the critically important, ultra-high-stakes organ transplant arena, systems such as this one can mean the difference between optimization and tragedy.

Shoulder Dystocia and Care Optimization

It is a maxim in the quality improvement area that the solution to a quality problem needs to match the need. But there are instances in which matching the solution to the need can be tricky. That was certainly true of the situation facing William Grobman, MD, and his colleagues in the labor and delivery area at Northwestern Memorial as they attempted to improve the quality of care given to delivering mothers whose babies were experiencing shoulder dystocia, a situation in which a baby's shoulders become stuck, impacted in the pelvis, preventing full vaginal delivery.

Grobman, an obstetrician/gynecologist with a subspecialty as a maternal fetal medicine doctor, says that while there are a number of maneuvers that can be used to facilitate the exit of the shoulders in shoulder dystocia situations, the process challenge involves several complicating factors. "Shoulder dystocia is some ways the perfect storm of problems in that it is terribly unpredictable," Grobman says. Not only does it only occur in about 1% of cases at Northwestern Memorial (he says the clinical literature cites a national range of between 0.2 and 2%); it is largely unpredictable with regard to other factors in a pregnancy and labor. Its relative rarity means that even at a hospital like Northwestern, which delivers 10,000 babies a year, Grobman notes that "Shoulder dystocia presents the problem that in a busy place like Northwestern, we would see this about 100 times a year. But a single individual physician or nurse might only see this once every few years." As a result, he observes, "Individual clinicians can't build up volume-based competency, in this area, and you can't build up an expert team, because you don't know when it'll happen, and you don't have time to find a specialized team when it does happen."

As a result, Grobman and his colleagues crafted a customized kind of response to the shoulder dystocia problem. "We instituted routinized responses," he says, "so that each person had some knowledge of how they would respond." In short, the doctor present, whether an attending or resident, will determine that a shoulder dystocia situation has presented itself, and then will announce that fact verbally. That announcement will trigger a series of steps that have been standardized and routinized by consensus, including the lead nurse initiating a series of actions, including starting a timer, mobilizing a team whose members are notified via a single call to a call tree, with representatives from anesthesia, pediatrics, and another attending who is on duty and available, and at least two nurses including the lead nurse (two nurses are normally present to begin with in any case).

This standardized process was initiated in 2006, and has been a success, Grobman notes, though because of the small volume of shoulder dystocia cases overall, at press time it remained early with regard to the amassing of data.

Qualitatively speaking, however, Grobman says he and his colleagues have been highly satisfied with the process and outcomes. "This is about systematizing processes, in situations that occur relatively rarely, unpredictably, and emergently," he says, "and about the challenge of systematizing a process in that case. We believe this gives our patients the chance to have better outcomes, and gives our physicians and nurses, who are incredibly skilled, the chance to use those skills most effectively."

A JOURNEY WITH A DESTINATION IN SIGHT

For all the professionals at Northwestern Memorial Hospital, the work being carried out at the hospital is a long-term investment in processes and supporting structures that they know will reap rewards over time, if the vision and strategies are right. "What's important is to know what the destination for our journey looks like," says Jay Anderson, vice-president of operations at Northwestern Memorial. "For us, that destination is to deliver safe, effective, timely, coordinated care to our patients. I'm biased, but I'd say, having a good process improvement architecture is a critical success factor, as is having the internal capability to do improvement. As institutions, that's historically not a built-in tool set." Finally, he adds, "Make sure to get the small wins. You just keep achieving small wins over and over, and learn what levers are successful, and extend those into additional environments."

NOTES

1 Cassano, Angela T. PharmD., "IV Medication Safety Software Implementation in a Multihospital Health System," *Hospital Pharmacy* 41, no. 2, February 2006. (2): 151–156.

6

Case Studies 7 to 9: Initiating Transformation on a Vast Scale

Leaders at Trinity Health, an integrated Catholic health system based in Novi, Michigan, but which serves patients in 44 hospitals in seven states, are attempting one of the broadest quality transformation efforts to date in the United States. Their work in a variety of areas, particularly with regard to standardizing clinical practices, is crossing new frontiers in eliminating unnecessary variation in clinical care (pp. 86–95).

An initiative created by clinician leaders at the Medical College of Georgia to improve stroke care outcomes is proving that information and medical technology, when skillfully combined with a fundamental rethinking of medical practice in a specific care area, and the desire to improve patients' outcomes, can help facilitate genuine breakthroughs in clinical care quality and outcomes (pp. 95–99).

Clinician leaders and executives at the 770-bed Tallahassee Memorial Hospital have leveraged their participation in the Pursuing Perfection program operated by the Boston-based Institute for Healthcare Improvement to dramatically reduce overall mortality rates at their organization. In fact, within three years of working to reduce overall mortality rates, Tallahassee Memorial Hospital clinicians were able to reduce their overall rates by an impressive nearly 31% (pp. 95–105).

CASE STUDY 7

Trinity Health Initiates Transformation on a Vast Scale

It is one thing to work to transform the quality and patient safety culture of a single hospital facility. It is quite another to initiate such work on a massive scale. Just ask the folks at Trinity Health, an integrated Catholic health system based in Novi, Michigan, but which serves patients in 44 hospitals across seven core states—Maryland, Ohio, Michigan, Indiana, Iowa, Idaho, and California (with its largest concentrations of facilities in Michigan and Iowa).

What Trinity leaders are attempting, if successful, would be one of the broadest quality transformation efforts to date. It's a significant ambition, and they know it. Their system-wide initiative's overall aims are nothing short of transforming the way care is delivered at Trinity Health's hospitals. Among the many elements in the initiative are the following:

- The development of standardized, evidence-based order sets, in a growing range of clinical areas
- The development of standardized clinical process workflows in a number of areas
- The development of a standardized approach to the measurement and evaluation of pain in post-hip and knee replacement patients and in inpatients in general
- The training of large numbers of clinician leaders, executives, and managers in Lean management and Six Sigma principles and strategies, in order to create a learning organization and internally develop a corps of change agents system-wide
- The system-wide-forward advance of a core electronic health record (EHR) for all facilities, as a key facilitator for process improvement, care quality enhancement, and patient safety
- The use of a spring forward-type approach, in which successful quality initiatives at individual hospitals within the system are then adopted system-wide, thus leveraging the work of clinician and staff leaders at individual organizations within the system

Above all, say Trinity leaders, at the core of their initiative lies a mission-driven, collaborative ambition to remake their system. Their "process excellence journey" began in 2003, and the health system's overall strategy was more formally defined by a strategic plan approved in July 2007. "Organiza-tionally, our culture is shifting from our ministry organizations working on their own, to more of a collaborative approach," says Tammy Merkel, director of process excellence for the health system. "And some of our work has been driven by the need to have standard processes supported by our information systems. So there has been much more sharing of data, collaboration, and looking at best practices together across the entire organization. And that's been the biggest cultural change."

Of course, moving out of silos of work and making system-wide prog-ress takes work—hard, coordinated work. "As this process has evolved, the ability to bring process improvement into the cultural transformation has solidified over time," says Laura Archbold, RN, process improvement spe-cialist-black belt, for Trinity Health. "Initially," she concedes, "the notion was that what we were doing was just a great idea, and everything would just fall into place because we had good intentions; and it didn't. So we've been putting in steps for process excellence training."

On a practical level, Archbold says, that has meant initiating extensive work in a number of Trinity Health facilities, as clinician groups have come together to map their care processes using their Lean management training. That work is currently in full swing, she reports. It is also becom-ing the basis for a whole range of process changes at individual hospitals that can then be leveraged by the entire health system, once they have been determined to have created best practices. This process-mapping proce-dure is now becoming the norm for initiating change in patient care pro-cesses in Trinity Health facilities.

Facing the Industry-Wide Challenge of Practice Pattern Variation

In committing to care quality transformation, the clinician leaders of Trinity Health have had to squarely face one of the most embedded and change-resistant problems in health care: the problem of fundamen-tal clinical practice pattern variation. Trinity Health leaders are very conscious of this. In fact, when asked what the biggest challenges to the advancement of their transformative work are, Merkel immediately cites the variation issue. "There are two aspects of this," she says, "looking at it from an individual-hospital perspective and from a systems perspective. From a systems perspective, you often have very wide variation across an organization. And the first challenge is figuring out what critical items you can fix that will impact most strongly the entire organization. We have 21 ministry organizations," she says, referring to the regional hospital cluster organizations within the overall system. "That's the first challenge."

"The second challenge," Merkel continues, "is that all the hospitals have their own process and culture. So you're taking into account a lot of variations, including in the ways they'll implement change. So there are challenges from a system level when you're looking to apply something so large. From the hospital perspective, the biggest challenge is implementing change. Change is very hard, because at the hospital level, they have to implement change, we just direct it. That's why it's critical that you have front-line associates involved, because their buy-in is critical."

In other words, the change leaders at Trinity Health are attempting to overcome a few different but interlocking problems that have bedeviled change agents in health care throughout its history:

- Individual clinician variation in patient care processes exists at every level of the U.S. health care system, all the way from differences between how any two individual clinicians work within even a single unit or service area, to unit-to-unit variation with a single hospital facility, to variation between hospitals in a multi-hospital system such as Trinity Health, to variation between unrelated organizations, to variation between different types of hospitals and patient care organizations (such as between academic medical centers and community hospitals, etc.).
- Attempting to create standardization within a single hospital facility is challenging enough; working across multi-facility organizations in different geographic locations has always been even more challenging.
- There has always been an industry-wide lack of evidence-based best practices, meaning that Trinity Health is attempting to innovate essentially from scratch.

These problems are ones that the Trinity Health change leaders are facing head-on. "At an individual hospital," Archbold says, "you can have multiple process improvement efforts going on, but if they're not synchronized, it's hard to optimize the results of those individual processes. Instead," she says, "if we can achieve synergy, so that they're working together, we can see greater improvement. Otherwise, you're not moving the needle." In order to best stimulate change, she says of the individual hospitals and regions, "We're trying to get them to organize around their values. Clearly, the integration of the work is really important for us as a system."

Standardizing and Optimizing Care for Orthopedic Surgery Patients

One example of an area in which the Trinity Health people have done intensive work to date both at the system level and via individual facilities has been in the area of standardizing and optimizing care for patients undergoing total hip and total knee replacements. These procedures are not only major sources of revenue and foci of activity for clinicians; they are also complex and multi-faceted—and were ripe for change.

As Merkel recalls it, "Initially, we had a vendor come in and pilot a program for us, and helped us develop a Care Transformation Team to create those protocols. We learned lessons from the vendor, and created a robust process for managing the care of an orthopedic patient for from the time they arrive until discharge. We did observations to try to understand the process, did measurement to understand what the value-added and non-value-added steps were; and we looked at the process to find out what this looked like through the eyes of the patients."

In fact, Trinity Health clinician leaders and change process leaders held patient dinners in which they quizzed patients about their experiences. The Trinity Health leaders videotaped the sessions. After six weeks of such work, Trinity Health clinicians—representing all types of clinicians involved in the care process, including surgeons, operating room directors, orthopedic nurses, recovery area managers, triage professionals, pharmacists, risk managers, and case managers—gathered for a four-day intensive session in April 2007 to begin the redesign of their orthopedic care processes. They methodically reviewed the data and the patient testimonials, and initiated intensive discussions about the orthopedic care process, including dialogue about hand-offs between different clinicians and staff members in the care process. "Everyone had a voice" in the discussion, Merkel emphasizes. And, she says, "There were 'aha!' moments that came out it, when we realized we didn't need to do certain things anymore, or that we could fix certain things."

During the rest of the conference, Trinity Health clinicians spent their time mapping the hip replacement and knee replacement processes, using

Lean concepts and tools. Working together, the group uncovered more than 380 problems in the care processes for the two procedures, as identified by current-state analysis. Some were very major, some minor, Merkel says.

Archbold shares examples of both types. "A minor problem," she says, "was that family members often brought the wrong kind of car, so that it was hard to get the patient in the car. A major problem was that our clinicians were unable to control patients' pain, and weren't able to design pain medication in association with their therapy. And though this was an elective procedure, they couldn't get all the paperwork done, all the clearances, before the hospital date, even though we knew they were coming four weeks in advance." That process issue of course further related to the ongoing challenge of more fully integrating physician practices into the health system's EHR.

In any case, a fundamental change in care management came out of that process, Merkel and Archbold report. And that is that, instead of clinicians following the old pattern of going by "day one, day two, day three," etc. plans, based on idealized concepts about patient progress that it turns out often don't match reality. Archbold says, "The patient now moves through those phases based on their own individual process and progress." Key phases of care include stabilization, rehabilitation, and discharge. And, perhaps paradoxically, by the very fact of standardizing care patterns and processes, that care can now be better customized to suit the needs of individual patients, Merkel adds.

Another example of the take-it-apart-and-rebuild-it approach being pursued at Trinity Health has involved medication reconciliation, reports J. Michael Kramer, MD, MBA, the organization's chief medical informatics officer (CMIO). "Two years ago," he recalls, "we brought people from across the system together, and they met for a week, and mapped the medication reconciliation process flow." Medication reconciliation is a pain point for many clinicians, he says, "but everyone recognized that no one is going to be able to improve the process unless we talk about this in the same way, with the same vocabulary. So we created a Lean map for medication reconciliation and used it to rework the process via a standardized approach." By its nature, using Lean to analyze and understand and then change processes that have evolved haphazardly over time requires the use of "very detailed, activity-based process workflows," Kramer says. "But to say that your process workflows are based on a Lean map, is very powerful. Because it means that your high-level thinking was right. Because your Lean principles flow all the way from that Lean map, to your specific process workflows."

The EHR's Centrality as a Facilitator and a Carrot

At this point, it is important to add to this discussion the relevance of Genesis, the Trinity Health-wide clinical information initiative that is building an electronic medical record across the whole of the organization in order to facilitate care quality and performance optimization. In the specific case of the development of standardized orthopedic care plans, Archbold reports that "We're building criteria and triggers into the electronic record. So when the patient accomplishes A, B, and C, they flip into the next phase."

More broadly, the work that Trinity Health clinicians are engaging in is being powered intensively by Genesis and its ongoing clinical information systems development. As Trinity Health's Web site explains it to patients and consumers:

> Trinity Health's vision to be a leader in improving health care delivery is demonstrated in its Genesis initiative. We are proud to be among the early leaders in the health care industry who are embracing leading-edge technology that supports the delivery of safe, high-quality patient care.
>
> Genesis puts the power of computerized clinical tools in the hands of its caregivers. In combination with our skilled, compassionate care, these tools will increase patient safety and the quality of care our patients receive. Notable industry studies show that computerized clinical systems offer substantial safety benefits.[1]

Meanwhile, Trinity Health executives recently confirmed the current scope of the Genesis project and the gains made so far in IT development across the Trinity Health system.

Key components include:

- Electronic health record (EHR), allowing for appropriate clinician access from any location, "thereby increasing coordination of care, enhancing clinical decisions, and reducing costly duplication of tests when handwritten records cannot be found"
- Computerized physician order entry (CPOE), which will "increas[e] the accuracy of the order, eliminating illegible handwritten orders, and reducing the potential for errors"
- ADE alert system: "Orders are cross-checked with a database to help physicians and pharmacists recognize potential drug interactions at

the point of clinical decision. ADE alert systems are operational at all Trinity Health facilities.

- Revenue management and supply chain management, to increase efficiencies and help reduce costs

As of January of 2008, the scope of Genesis was as follows:

- Phased clinical and revenue cycle system implementation at 31 hospitals
- Data repository currently maintains records for more than 5.9 million patients
- Overall rate of 70% for computerized provider order entry, well above expected rates
- 228,000 patient charts accessed daily
- 445,000 new orders processed daily
- Average number of Cerner users logged on at any given time daily: 6,000
- Average number of HealthQuest users daily: 1,088
- 180 evidence-based order sets developed
- 367 active clinical rules
- 311 clinical documentation forms
- 35 physician-structured documentation templates
- Major software vendors: Cerner (clinical), McKesson (revenue cycle), and Lawson (supply chain management)

Of the massive quality improvement and clinical IT development work taking place at Trinity Health, Kramer says that "There's clearly been a recognition that the health care system is broken, and that clarity about the processes of care is limited. I think the transformational nature of this work is that we're going to break and redesign the care process in its entirety. I don't know a lot of people who want to hold on to the traditional, paper-based, hierarchical models," he says.

Kramer, one of several key leaders of Project Genesis, sees progress towards automation both as a facilitator of change and as a benefit that can help achieve buy-in among clinicians to work towards further change. "We do a lot of work around creating messages around transformation," he says. Indeed, Kramer notes, "Going into our hospitals and helping clinician leaders and executives construct a message for their organization, is the first step in cultural change"—with IT innovation an integral element in the discussion. "So in an organization without an EMR, we'll say, 'OK, we're going to talk about safety, or transcriptional errors.'" As a result, he says, the dialogue around change becomes an integrated discussion about broad goals and also about the means to reach those goals, including Project Genesis and automation.

Inevitably, Kramer says, there is an intermingling of strategic and clinical objectives and activity with technology objectives and advancement. For example, he says, "St. Joseph Mercy Oakland, in Pontiac, Michigan, wants to be a leader. They've developed a stroke network, a center of excellence, for stroke. They brought the rounding robots in, so this robot drives up to the bedside. It's cool technology. But," he quickly adds, "one of the things that they recognized is that although they'd put in these cool robots, they had not provided the order sets; so, what is the evidence-based information to the transformation? How do I make sure the thrombolytics are done right?"

With the help of the right technologies, Kramer says, individual hospital organizations within Trinity Health are pioneering various innovations, which can then be leveraged system-wide once they've been adopted as best practices. So, for example, going back to the stroke care example, he reports that St. Joseph Mercy Oakland clinicians, through their work in that area, have "established themselves as leaders in stroke care."

How does all this tie together? For Kramer, all the streams of thought and activity meet around the concept of the social contract with regard to working in an individual hospital facility within a large, diverse multi-hospital system spread across several states. "When you have a system like ours, with 31 hospitals that will be on a standard system, you lose [operational] autonomy," he concedes. "So one of the things we've offered as terms of engagement has been that people would retain some level of autonomy in decision-making. If you build an organizational structure in which some things will be imposed on hospitals, but you allow individual hospitals to create autonomy through independent quality work, that's an important element in engagement. So they've created the evidence-based order sets" for stroke care at St. Joseph Mercy Oakland, and in the process, clinician leaders at that hospital have distinguished themselves within the Trinity Health family, while at the same time seeding innovation for the whole system.

Lessons Learned

Trinity Health's leaders fully recognize the enormity of the task they are taking on, which is nothing less than reinventing patient care processes across a vast multi-hospital system spread out over seven states. Indeed, they understand that what they are attempting could be seen by some as a microcosm of what is being attempted nationwide with regard to the transformative quality revolution. And the work involved is really hard. But they also believe that keeping their collective "eyes on the prize" could bring them the ultimate rewards they seek, over time.

"That is the whole premise behind process excellence, that if you can standardize the process, then you can use your creativity as you care for the patient," says Tammy Merkel. The biggest lesson learned from the development of the new, standardized care plans for the orthopedic procedures, along with the concomitant development of a standardized pain evaluation scale, is that "What was most exciting was when you started to see the team realize that they were more similar than different," though they came from different hospital facilities, "and that they could create a more standardized process, and that that could help them be more flexible in terms of meeting individual patients' needs. Once they realized that, and realized that they were designing a process to focus on the patient, they were very excited. Because that's why nurses went into nursing. And poor processes were getting in their way; this takes out a lot of those bottlenecks and barriers."

Archbold adds that, "To me, the most impressive thing was just the power of the team. Because we gave them 48 feet of blank wall, and their expertise and experiences, and said, design a total joint care program, and they came up with a plan that met every requirement for JCAHO [the Oakbrook Terrace, Ill.-based Joint Commission on Accreditation of Healthcare Organizations], the national safety goals, every coding requirement, and they created a plan that met everyone's expectations, and the team was very proud and pleased with what they did."

What do the Trinity Health leaders believe that the progress at their organization to date says about the potential for the transformative quality efforts to succeed more generally?

"I go back to some of the foundations of Lean, including empowering the front-line associates and trusting them to do what's right, and giving them the tools to know how to address problems when they come their way," says Merkel. "If we can put that into the culture, and build processes and structures to support that, I think that those who say it can't be done would take a different view. I've worked as an industrial engineer in hospitals, and I've had the opportunity to observe processes, and some of the processes we have right now are very difficult and cumbersome."

Even ostensibly "simple" processes such as distributing medications often turn out to be highly problematic, Merkel says. "But if front-line people have the ability to suggest change, and are empowered to fix the problems in front of them, you can create a different culture. What we have to do is to make the process less cumbersome," she emphasizes. It is through the redesigning of core patient care processes that real gains can be made, she stresses. It is only then that the health care system can get beyond current operating difficulties, such as the oft-cited problem of 60% of nurses' time being spent on non-value-added tasks and chores.

In order to get to the level at which such conditions can be fundamentally altered, Archbold says, "There needs to be a lot of training. Our mid-level managers right now aren't used to managing empowered people. Everyone needs to learn to work in this new environment to make it work. So I think the very best thing we could do when talking to our staff is to simply ask, what would you do? It's a very empowering step. It shows that they're valued, and we can move on from there. And then we have to show them the trust and allow them to do it. But they need to look both upstream and downstream for change."

In the end, say Trinity Health executives, the processes of furthering process improvement, of implementing facilitative technology, and of furthering cultural change, all merge together into an overall drive towards organizational transformation, with every aspect supporting the others. "We've made this investment" in patient care process change and in technology, Kramer says. "We know what we want, and we don't want to go back. And that's part of the cultural transformation that has to occur; you have to build those messages, build your leadership, build those changes. As a result, there is a positive improvement culture here now."

NOTES

1. http://www.trinity-health.org/initiatives/genesis.shtml.

CASE STUDY 8

Improving Stroke Outcomes in Rural Health Care Markets

Technology alone is never a panacea for patient care problems; but, when combined with a fundamental rethinking of medical practice in a specific care area, and the desire to improve patients' outcomes, the intelligent use of information and medical technology can help facilitate genuine break-throughs in clinical care quality and patient outcomes.

That's what has happened in the area of acute stroke care treatment, among a small but growing coterie of hospitals and health systems in several states. Physician leaders at those organizations are coupling a brand-new, Web-based technology with a new approach to treating patients presenting with acute stroke symptoms, and are in the process saving lives, saving brain function, and vastly improving the odds that patients living in remote rural areas in Georgia, Florida, South Carolina, and New York (and soon California and Texas as well) will survive their strokes and approach their maximal potential post-stroke functionality.

Historically, patients living in very remote rural areas who experienced acute stroke symptoms had poor outcomes, for a complex set of reasons. Not only were those patients living far from the big hospitals with sophisticated stroke care and neurologists and neurosurgeons on staff; transporting them to those hospitals was cumbersome and difficult, and most of all, time-consuming. Often, precious minutes and even hours were lost in transporting the patients to those hospitals for the best evaluation and treatment possible (whether by ambulance or helicopter). Meanwhile, the small, rural hospitals nearer to them had bare-bones emergency rooms staffed only by emergency physicians and nurses without specific stroke evaluation and treatment skills. Some also lacked the CT and MRI scanning equipment needed as well. What's more, the one FDA-approved medication to date that has shown excellent results in breaking up the blood clots that lead to and aggravate ischemic strokes, tissue plasminogen activator, or tPA, must be administered within three hours of the onset of acute stroke symptoms. Because of the geographic challenges involved, the vast majority of residents of remote, rural areas in the United States rarely are in a position to be given tPA in time. Indeed, nationwide, fewer than 2% of stroke patients are given tPA.

It was with all these factors in mind that David Hess, MD, professor and chairman of the Department of Neurology at the Medical College of Georgia (MCG), in Augusta, began to try to tackle the stroke care challenge at the organization's flagship hospital facility, the 478-bed MCG Medical Center, when he arrived at MCG as chairman of neurology in 2000. "One of the issues that drove us forward was that it was becoming increasingly obvious to us in the late 1990s and early years of this decade that our ability to impact acute stroke care was very limited, because a chart review showed that two-thirds of our patients had presented first at outlying emergency rooms," he says. "And often, the delay was six or more hours. We'd get a telephone call from an emergency physician saying, help, I can't fully treat this patient, so the patient would end up arriving at the major medical center three hours after the onset of stroke, whether by ground ambulance or by helicopter. What's more," he says, "the process was inefficient, because sometimes you were transferring patients who aren't severe, and who would get better with guidance. So we never thought that the 'evaluate telephone and transfer' approach was a good protocol." The service area for the organization includes extremely remote, backwoods-rural areas in northeastern and eastern Georgia, he notes, with a relatively poor and isolated population, and where most of the local hospitals are very small, critical-access facilities, many with 25 to 50 beds and tiny clinical staffs, usually without any specialists.

Fortuitously, a neurology fellow who had an extra year on his hands (while the post-medical student waited for his wife to complete her medical school training) was able to use his extra time researching the possibility of creating some sort of telemedicine-based acute stroke care program for MCG. (Georgia has had a statewide telemedicine program in place since the late 1990s, Hess says, but he adds that it is "a cumbersome system with technology that was very difficult to use.") After extensive research and numerous professional and personal connections falling into place, MCG was able to pilot a telestroke program that involves the use of a video camera on a cart, and which has since then been commercialized by the Augusta, Georgia-based startup IT firm REACH Call, Inc.

Essentially, the model that the MCG folks created, and that is being replicated outside of Georgia where the service is being introduced, involves the establishment of a hub-and-spoke system, with a comprehensive stroke center (MCG Medical Center, in Georgia) as its hub. The two "spokes" of the system are the network of rural hospitals and physician offices and homes (neurologists and neurosurgeons). When a patient arrives at a rural hospital in the network presenting with stroke symptoms, the clinicians at that hospital use a REACH cart to initiate a consult request with a physician affiliated with the hub hospital of the network. The cart uses non-proprietary, off-the-shelf components, including a laptop, monitor, keyboard, mouse, and camera. Spoke hospital ER staff can use the Web browser running on the laptop embedded in the cart to register the patient and to request a consult with a remote affiliated physician. That specialist can then view the patient remotely and perform a clinical assessment, and, very importantly, the specialist can guide the rural hospital ER clinicians through the administration of tPA, if appropriate; or through the determination to transport, or discharge, the patient, as appropriate.

Georgia's hub-and-spoke system now involves 10 rural hospitals, all linked to MCG and to affiliated neurologists and neurosurgeons via the REACH Call Web-based technology. On average, Hess says, about half of the patients who present at the spoke hospitals in the system are ultimately transferred to MCG, and the other half remain at the spoke hospitals. In either case, the administration of tPA has increased dramatically for those patients, who would virtually never have received the life-saving drug before the initiation of the program.

The core lesson in this advance? Hess says it's quite clear. "What we can do with web-based telestroke systems is that we can really remove the geographic penalty that many people throughout the United States and the world are under. What's hard to get across to people is how medicine has changed. In the past, most hospitals could demand that doctors come to their ER and practice. But that isn't happening anymore. Most hospitals have a lot of trouble with specialist call. You can't get specialists out to those rural hospitals, and the hospitals are so geographically far-flung that you can't even get people to drive there." But, as has been demonstrated by MCG's program, the intelligent, strategic use of a Web-based tool for evaluation and consult purposes, deployed within the context of a well-planned hub-and-spoke network system, can dramatically improve patient outcomes.

Western New York Creates Its Own Network

The need to establish networks similar to MCG's extends far beyond Georgia; fortunately, the service model created there is being successfully replicated elsewhere. In western New York, the five-hospital Kaleida Health (whose flagship is the 511-bed Buffalo General Hospital) went live with its own hub-and-spoke system (with 11 "spoke" rural hospitals), also utilizing the REACH Call technology, in November 2006.

Although at the time of the writing of this book it was too early to be able to present detailed outcomes data, the results so far have been highly satisfactory, says Leo Nelson "Nick" Hopkins, MD, chief of neurosurgery for Kaleida Health, and a leader of the program. "If you have a patient with a limited block and if you can open up that block," Hopkins explains, "it's almost like flipping a switch [inside that patient]. Within minutes, if the artery can be opened and the brain is still viable, the patient can start functioning almost immediately. An added factor, he says, is the ease of use of the technology (which is very inexpensive, requiring only the use of a $6,000 telemedicine cart and high-speed Internet connectivity, plus the cost of the monthly subscription to the REACH Call service, which runs about $4,500 per month on average for hub hospitals and about $2,500 for spoke hospitals, according to REACH Call executives).

"The technology is quite simple but very sophisticated," Hopkins says. "You can zoom in to see the patient quite clearly. You can talk with the emergency room patients and even the patient, so it's pretty straightforward. And the patient's demographics are all entered into the REACH system before you start the consult—time of onset, patient's medications, patient's history, etc. And when you go through the NIH stroke scale exam, you come up with a stroke scale reading, and whether or not and how to treat the patient at the point."

This technology-facilitated advance has come along at a meaningful time in the history of stroke treatment, Hopkins says. "It used to be that if a stroke patient came into a rural ER," he says, "One of two things might happen. The patient might simply be left there with the patient's primary care physician managing the stroke, which really means supporting care; or the ER physician might call his favorite referral center, and the patient might be transferred. Years ago, there wasn't a whole lot of benefit to transferring; there wasn't a whole lot we could do. Today," he notes, "there are a lot of things we can do, especially with regard to sophisticated imaging to determine what parts of the brain are viable; we also have more options than just one drug." But the success of a system like this one also requires some proselytizing on the part of the leaders of any program like this, in order to convince rural ER physicians of the value of such a program and gain their participation in it.

The success of this hub-and-spoke model of IT-assisted stroke care has been highly gratifying, says MCG's Hess. "To me," he says, "the patients win, the outlying hospitals win, and we win. And with regard to the outlying hospitals, it cements our relationship with them." The broader issue of how networks such as MCG Medical Center's and Kaleida's will be financed in the future as they become more broadly adopted remains an unanswered question, he concedes.

But what is evident from the success of these networks, say MCG's Hess and Kaleida's Hopkins, is that, applied intelligently, a combination of smart technology and the right service model can shift paradigms in specialty care in medicine. Clearly, the potential to transform the stroke care paradigm nationwide exists, to the potential benefit of countless patients every year.

CASE STUDY 9

Tallahassee Memorial: Dramatic Improvements in Mortality Rates, Plus Transparency for the Community

The Pursuing Perfection program operated by the Boston-based Institute for Healthcare Improvement has helped numerous hospitals and health systems to improve their clinical quality and patient safety outcomes. Among the more noteworthy turnaround stories comes one out of Florida, where clinician leaders and executives at Tallahassee Memorial Hospital, the 770-bed community hospital that is the core inpatient component of Tallahassee Memorial HealthCare, have dramatically reduced overall mortality rates at their organization. In fact, within three years of working to reduce overall mortality rates, Tallahassee Memorial Hospital clinicians were able to reduce their overall rates by an impressive nearly 31%.

The path toward those improvements began with some shocking revelations, says Barbara MacArthur, RN, MN, vice-president and chief nursing officer at Tallahassee Memorial Hospital. "Back in early 2000," MacArthur recalls, "we recognized that there were problems—that it was time to really become strategic in our outcomes work. Now, I don't think that that's particularly unique to us," she adds. But when the initial group of hospitals participating in the IHI program began to look at a variety of outcomes measures around mortality, the Tallahassee Memorial leaders were shocked to learn that by one key measure, referred to as "adjusted mortality," their organization's score was very high; in fact, it was one of the highest among the group of 12 Pursuing Perfection grantee hospitals in the United States (two foreign hospitals were also participants). "If you look at the way that metric works, it speaks to the expected number of deaths you might have given your hospital's patient population," MacArthur explains. "If you had the expected number, your score would be 100. But our score was 130 or so, a horrible score. So that was a huge wake-up call for us."

At the outset, MacArthur says, "The concept of perfection was a notion we really had to grapple with. Can you really expect perfect care? That was a philosophical question attached to the grant. And the grant came out of the IOM reports, *To Err Is Human,* and *Crossing the Quality Chasm.* And we struggled with whether you could expect perfect care." She says of Donald Berwick, MD, IHI's president and CEO, that "Don Berwick came and visited us, and he said, 'Of course you can expect perfection, particularly if it's your mother who you'd be caring for. And would you be willing to say publicly that you expect imperfect care? Of course not.' So off we went to work."

What happened next, MacArthur says, offers a key insight into Tallahassee Memorial's success in their clinical quality transformation work. "I've been asked any number of times what the greatest learning piece was from the grant, and what has carried us through the process" of change, she says. "And the biggest learning piece for all of us was achieving small, rapid measures of change, getting quick gains. Typically, in the past," she says, "hospitals did enormous amounts of retroactive review of many-quarters-old, and sometimes years-old, data, and then wondered why things couldn't be made better. So one of the phrases we coined was, 'What can you do by Tuesday?'" In other words, it was a combination of commitment to move rapidly, using current data, to obtain quick wins that could encourage front-line caregivers, that helped spur broader change in Tallahassee.

With that working philosophy in place, MacArthur and her colleagues went to work. One of the first aspects they tackled was the measure of what is often referred to as "door-to-dilation" for heart attack patients with an occluded vessel. "We knew that if you could get a patient dilated within 90 minutes or less, you could lower mortality significantly," MacArthur says. "That means, for example, that if a patient crosses the threshold of your emergency room in an ambulance or walks in, you really must obtain an electrocardiogram (EKG) on that patient within 10 minutes or less, because the EKG starts the roadmap, starts the cascade" of care for such a patient. The Tallahassee Memorial clinicians found that the average time from emergency department (ED) entry to EKG was initially 36 minutes. Why? A host of very specific practical obstacles had been standing in the way, including the location of the EKG technicians four floors away from the ED. Making very simple changes, including moving the EKG techs to the same floor as the ED, lowered that 36-minute average to seven minutes.

Some of the remaining obstacles to door-to-dilation for heart attack patients turned out to stem from simple misunderstandings, yet clearly with major patient outcome consequences. For example, MacArthur says, there was the "urban myth" that if a patient was under the care of a private-practice physician, that the hospital was required to telephone the cardiologist before it phoned the patient's primary care physician. That assumption turned out to be completely untrue and it empowered the ED physicians to make definitive clinical decisions was another element in drawing down the overall door-to-dilation time for heart attack patients. Even such practical considerations as changing staff parking rules to allow cardiac catheterization lab staff members to park next to the main building contributed to the overall change.

As progress was made (in steps) in this area, MacArthur says, her team of change agents celebrated every incremental step forward. "The night we did our first EKG in five minutes, we celebrated Mary the EKG tech the next day," she recalls. And within a couple of months, the average had been lowered to a consistent seven minutes.

The lesson learned in that regard? "You have to look at the whole cascade of events and break it down into small, analyzable steps, because they become the rate-determining element in all this, in the cascade" of patient care delivery steps, MacArthur says. "And you don't have to measure those steps over a long period of time; you just make the change and move forward, you move on. And if it doesn't work, you haven't invested an enormous effort in it."

Rapid-Response Teams

Another area that MacArthur and her colleagues tackled was in averting full-blown strokes in patients already in med-surg beds in the hospital. Soon after beginning their Pursuing Perfection work, they adopted a practice being applied in several Pursuing Perfection hospitals, which was to create teams of intensive care unit (ICU) nurses with specialized skills and experience. Armed with printed business-type cards handed out to staff, any clinician or staff member (usually a floor nurse) can call the hospital's Stroke Team hotline number through the hospital's operator, and a Stroke Team member will show up and assist in the evaluation of a patient who might possibly be undergoing a stroke.

Another innovation that has added significantly to the progress in bringing down mortality rates has been the adoption of multidisciplinary rounds. These are led by Richard MacArthur, MD, the hospital's coordinator of evidence-based care. Dr. MacArthur (who also happens to be Nurse MacArthur's spouse) is a cardiac surgeon by background; but in the past three years, he has transitioned into this full-time position, making rounds with fellow physicians, and with nurses, case managers, clinical pharmacists, and physical therapists, discussing in multi-disciplinary meetings the cases of patients who have been inpatients for more than four days. The rounding takes only about a half-hour each time it is performed, but has produced dramatic results in terms of rapid interventions in care plans and treatment, all those involved say.

In addition to all these elements, Richard MacArthur also cites the development of standardized order sets as yet another element contributing to overall outcomes improvement at Tallahassee Memorial Hospital. It has been hard work, but highly rewarding, he says, to have helped to reduce the unnecessary variation in order sets. "There were 26 different order sets in orthopedics when I started trying to get physicians to practice evidence-based medicine, and they were somewhat similar," he recalls. "And those 26 different order sets were for just 22 orthopedists. It was a quagmire" of unnecessary practice variation, he adds.

Still, MacArthur says, it's clear that there is enough evidence in the clinical literature in a number of areas to support far broader standardization of care approaches by physicians. The challenge? "Physician culture is always very slow to change," he says. "Physicians tend to get locked into things they like to do, are familiar with, and are comfortable with. They don't like to be told what to do. On the other hand, it's possible to make things simple for them, so that they don't have to redo things all the time. Using the protocols developed at Tallahassee Memorial, he notes, "The doctor sits down and types in the diagnosis, and an order set comes up."

Overcoming physician resistance to standardization also requires some persuasion with regard to what it will mean for them as individuals. "They all say, 'I don't want to do cookbook medicine,'" Dr. MacArthur says, "but the truth is, they don't want to do *other people's* cookbook medicine; they want to do *their own*. We just have to tell them, well, here's your cookbook."

Of course, this standardization improves the entire process of care delivery as things move downstream from physicians to other clinicians in the care process, MacArthur notes. "The nurses, pharmacists, and respiratory therapists all want standard order sets, too, so that they don't have to memorize every single doctor's way of doing things," he says. "And over time, in the pharmacy, you can reduce your storage shelves. Especially at a place like ours, with young nurses coming into the system, if they know they'll always see the same order sets, they'll become more familiar, and then be less likely to make mistakes."

Information technology has clearly been a facilitator for the progress made so far, says Mary Bland, RN, vice-president and CIO. "My team continues to be very involved," Bland says. "We have ongoing projects with the clinical side of the house." IT, she notes, has also worked rapidly to implement technology to support clinician efforts. "For instance," she says, "with regard to the stroke program, when we have high-risk patients coming in with a certain diagnosis, and the clinicians need to make sure that they are given aspirin or beta blockers upon admission or at discharge, the system will provide an alert to do that."

Analysts who did much of the necessary number crunching to support the various initiatives described above definitely relied on the tools of automation to do the statistical analysis required, she adds.

CEO Support at Hand

The intensive clinical care quality improvement work that clinicians have been leading to date at Tallahassee Memorial Hospital would not have been possible without very strong executive management and board support, Barbara MacArthur and Richard MacArthur agree. Both cite the leadership of Mark O'Bryant, the Tallahassee organization's president and CEO for the past several years, as a key element in the organization's forward movement on quality and safety improvement.

"We're not yet where we want to be," says O'Bryant. "But we've been pretty successful at defining a vision that everyone can understand and embrace. And we've been focusing on creating a sense of ownership across the entire organization, and frankly even across our community." Indeed, he notes, "When we created a strategic plan, it was inclusive of all the stakeholder groups, from the patient population to the business leaders and other purchasers and the health insurers, to the staff. And we created the strategic plan as a living document. And once you've created the strategic plan, you then have to create the belief that you can accomplish it."

In addition, O'Bryant says, the entire organization continues to do what Barbara MacArthur and her team did with regard to door-to-dilation for occluded-vessel heart attack patients—every time a step towards progress has been made, it's been recognized by the organization. "As we've made improvements, we've recognized and celebrated them with events, to create a sense of ownership," he says. "Now I can't say that everybody completely bought into the organization; so as a result, we've had to make some changes" to staffing. But most staff have accepted and embraced the change movement, and that has made all the difference.

Barbara MacArthur notes that a few additional elements have factored into the cultural shift that has taken place at the Tallahassee Memorial organization. "Four years ago, as we were nearing the end of the first or second phase of Pursuing Perfection, the hospital underwent a significant change in leadership. A bright, young CEO came in," she says, referring to O'Bryant. "The previous CEO had been here 15-plus years. And a new CMO and a new CNO and a new COO were all named; I was the new CNO." So the broad leadership change that took place apart from the quality effort helped invigorate the quality transformation with bold, new energy.

In addition, MacArthur recalls, the local newspaper, the *Tallahassee Democrat*, openly called for a change in hospital leadership at Tallahassee Memorial in a front-page Sunday editorial in early 2003, a development she calls "pretty interesting, considering that we're a private hospital." In any case, she also recalls, "The community at that time pretty much said, we want to love this hospital, and it isn't a very lovable hospital right now."

In other words, when put together, these several elements—natural leadership turnover and change; pressure from the hospital's community; and challenging data coming out of participation in the IHI grantee program—all helped to create the "burning platform" for change that helped to propel the Tallahassee Memorial organization forward, its clinician and executive leaders agree.

Of course, in order to achieve the transformation that the Tallahassee Memorial folks are working to achieve, "You have to have a critical mass of strong operational people," Barbara MacArthur notes. "Because you may be very well-intentioned, but what you need is people who can get it done; and the leadership issue is key. The transparency piece is huge, too, because your community and staff support you. And you share the good news and the not-so-good news. And everybody gets to relish the improvement."

What's up next at the Tallahassee Memorial organization? The organization's leaders are reevaluating their strategic plan for potential future modifications, MacArthur notes. O'Bryant says, "We will continue to put more measurements in place and to look at outcomes programs from across the country. Our goal," he adds, "is to become a recognized leader in quality, and to grow in transparency. There's not only a sense here that we can become that, but now, there's a real sense that we *will* become that. It's heartening. The biggest risk," he adds, "is that a sense of complacency can set in. So we need to make sure that we don't just fall into a comfortable 'glide' path. The truth is," he concludes, "now is the time to build on the momentum we've achieved and to keep going. We should appreciate that we have gotten better, but that we still have room to improve. If anyone who tells me that they and their organization are now perfect in terms of quality, frankly, I would say they and their organization are delusional. So the challenge is to continue to keep constantly improving. And that's where the transparency comes in."

7

Case Studies 10 to 11: Creating Clinical Cultures of Partnership

Clinician leaders at the University of Rochester (NY) Medical Center have unlocked an opportunity for care quality improvement that is being looked at by hospitals across the country, as they've pioneered the development of a clinical pharmacist program in their emergency department (pp. 107–110).

A strongly patient-centric approach to creating change has been a critical success factor in the work of clinician leaders at Wheaton Franciscan Healthcare-St. Joseph, a 538-bed hospital in Milwaukee, Wisconsin, whose wave of cultural change is bringing about clinical quality improvement based on collaboration among all the hospital's internal stakeholders, and rippling out across the entire 16-hospital Wheaton Franciscan Healthcare system (pp. 111–117).

CASE STUDY 10

The University of Rochester Medical Center's ED Clinical Pharmacy Program Reduces Medication Errors

It is universally understood that the working environment in any hospital emergency department (ED) is one fraught with potential medical errors. Much of the communication is verbal in nature; speed and timing are of the absolute essence; a significant proportion of the patient caseload at any time involves highly urgent care needs; and there is less time for the kinds of thorough documentation and inter-disciplinary communication that are easier to achieve in non-urgent environments in which patients' care has been planned in advance.

At the confluence of all these challenges, clinician leaders at the 739-bed University of Rochester Medical Center in Rochester (URMC), New York, have unlocked an opportunity for care quality improvement that is being looked at by hospitals across the country. One clinical pharmacist working in the 120-bed URMC emergency department, in concert with physician leaders, in early 2001 established a pioneering program to place at least one full-time clinical pharmacist in the ED, where that pharmacist would be available across an entire shift at a time to intervene clinically and support the multidisciplinary care team, in order to prevent medication errors, adjust medications, and perform other important tasks. The results have been highly encouraging, and point to the potential to reduce errors and improve care across the emergency department.

Daniel P. Hays, PharmD, a clinical pharmacy specialist, and Rollin J. "Terry" Fairbanks, MD, an assistant professor of emergency medicine and emergency physician, have been the change leaders at URMC. In fact, it all began with Hays's clinical pharmacy internship. "One of my first clinical rotations in doing my PharmD was in an ED in Minneapolis, and I saw the potential there for pharmacy rotations in the ED," Hays recalls. "I looked at the multitude of patients in the ED, the multitude of medications patients are on, and the need to turn care steps around quickly, and to get as much information as possible out of patients so that they could go on to their next step in the care process," Hays says. As a result, he says, he came to the conclusion that having a pharmacist posted in the ED made sense with regard to every aspect of patient care quality improvement and patient throughput.

"Emergency medicine is a unique environment in the medical field," adds Fairbanks. "We're treating patients in a situation in which we don't know their correct medication record or history; we don't know a lot about them. Secondly, there is less of a built-in protection program for medication in the ED. For instance, if you're a patient on a medical floor or ICU, most of your medications are routinely ordered by doctors. And as part of that process, a medication order goes down to the pharmacy, where they check the medication against their medication list, check it for dosage, issues such as kidney function, etc.; and then when the medication arrives on the floor, it is checked by nurses. In the ED, nearly all medications are urgent meds that aren't reviewed or dispensed by the pharmacy."

For all those reasons, Fairbanks was highly supportive when Hays proposed the establishment of an accredited residency program for pharmacists specializing in emergency medicine. As of early 2008, URMC was only one of two hospitals in the United States to offer a residency program specifically in emergency medicine clinical pharmacy (the other is the Detroit Receiving Hospital in Detroit). In addition, Fairbanks says, only 3% of emergency departments have dedicated ED pharmacists at present.

Currently, URMC's ED now has two full-time positions in clinical pharmacy, though one is open due to a maternity leave. Meanwhile, Hays is able to work four successive 12-hour shifts every week in the ED. His day is never routine, he says. Instead, he checks in on patients in the ED, beginning with the most acute patients first, and reviews their status and charts along with a pharmacy resident who accompanies him. Those clinical pharmacy residents working in the program work in the ED in the context of a six-month mentorship in ED clinical pharmacy. What kinds of issues crop up? "Everything from patients who may have a penicillin allergy but who have had penicillin or a penicillin-like cousin drug ordered for them, to patients who are on medications inappropriate for their renal function, to patients who have had medications ordered that are inappropriate to their clinical situation. Perhaps 5 to 10% of orders are inappropriate," he reports.

In terms of the amount of time involved, Fairbanks notes that Hays is spending the bulk of his time consulting with physicians who approach him before writing a medication order that would be inappropriate. "I call him all the time and say, 'Hey, Dan, I have a patient who's on six medications, and I need to give him an antibiotic.' Or, I come to him to ask about heparin dosing. He really is a clinical adviser. We performed an internal study, and found that we are averting potential adverse events," he adds, "because we're coming to him first."

Ultimately, the success of the program, and the URMC physicians' satisfaction with it, derives from the opportunity for physicians and nurses to involve clinical pharmacists in the fast-paced realm of patient care at the bedside in the ED. "From my standpoint as an emergency physician, I find that when we're dealing with emergency situations where a patient is critically ill or injured, that having a pharmacist as a member of the team or at the bedside is a big plus," Fairbanks says. "Things go faster in terms of medications, and the pharmacists help us deliver the right medications faster. For example, we may be focused on a patient's major chest trauma and we're trying to work out their airway, and Dan may say, 'Why don't we give this patient some fentanyl, because he's in a lot of pain?' He helps advise on appropriate medications, anticipate appropriate medications, and help us get ready faster."

Meanwhile, Hays adds that for the clinical pharmacist, knowing that his very presence in the ED helps to reduce medication errors, and being given the opportunity not only to work at the bedside with physicians and nurses on medication problems, but also to review medication errors monthly with the ED physicians, gives him great professional satisfaction as a pharmacy professional.

Is the URMC model of ED clinical pharmacy practice replicable to other patient care organizations? Absolutely, say Hays and Fairbanks. The key, Hays says, is that it is important to follow a "be-visible, be-available model. I carry a wireless phone," he notes, "and we post signs showing when the clinical pharmacist is on and off duty in the ED. When fully staffed, we cover 80 hours a week," he adds, "focusing on the prime-time hours, which in Rochester run between about 11 AM to about 9 PM most weekdays, though they will naturally vary by city," he notes.

URMC's design for the ED clinical pharmacy program was so noteworthy that it won the 2005 ASHP Best Practices Award from the Bethesda, Maryland-based American Society of Health-System Pharmacists, specifically for the program's work in trauma resuscitation cases. Of the work that went into the program, Cynthia Brennan, PhD, the ASHP's president, said in a September 2007 URMC press release, "Patients in the ED often are taking multiple medications and present complex medical challenges. As such, these patients need and deserve high quality care from pharmacists who are medication-use experts."[1]

Also, what should clinician leaders and executives at other organizations know about the benefits of this kind of program? "That it is really a huge improvement in all aspects of patient care," Hays reflects. "I've had faculty who've tried to model their work schedule after mine, in order to be working in the ED when the clinical pharmacist is there. A couple of our physicians have requested to only work when I work."

NOTES

1. "Strong Mentors Pharmacists Seeking to Fill Emergency Department Role." University of Rochester Medical Center press release, September 17, 2007. (accessed July 2008)

CASE STUDY 11

Wheaton Franciscan Healthcare
Creates a Culture of Partnership

Wheaton Franciscan Healthcare-St. Joseph, a 538-bed hospital in Milwaukee, Wisconsin, and a member of the Wheaton-Franciscan Healthcare system, has been the site of a wave of cultural change, a wave that is bringing about clinical quality improvement based on collaboration among all the hospital's internal stakeholders, and rippling out across the entire Wheaton, Illinois-based Wheaton Franciscan Healthcare system, whose 16 hospital facilities are spread across Wisconsin, Iowa and Illinois.

The key, say the organization's clinician leaders, has been the patient-centric approach they have taken to creating change.

Stephen Cardamone, MD, who had been a regional medical executive for Wheaton-Franciscan's Iowa hospitals for seven years, in January 2007, became chief medical officer for the entire system. Cardamone says that physicians have come around to the collaborative approach Wheaton-Franciscan leaders have been impressing upon the culture, "because we have been patient-centric." What's more, physicians have been involved from the very start with nurses, pharmacists, and other clinicians in defining the vision for quality transformation in the organization, and moving to create the called-for changes.

At the time that interviews were done for this book, Cardamone had been in his position as system CMO for just 14 months. But he and his fellow clinician leaders say that early progress made at St. Joseph's in Milwaukee is helping to infuse the entire system, spread out across Wisconsin, Illinois, and Iowa, with a transformative spirit.

Until a couple of years ago, Cardamone says, "Our system functioned more regionally, if you will. But," he adds quickly, "we're very much now working in an integrated fashion to function as a system. And that under-scores our commitment to the idea that patients can access the same level of quality and effectiveness in any hospital in the system. To that end, we've really tried to accelerate our performance improvement programs; and in that regard, we've benefited from high-intensity programs like those at St. Joseph's, that have involved rapid-cycle improvement and process redesign." What's more, he says, several Wheaton-Franciscan hospitals in Wisconsin and Iowa, including St. Joseph's in Milwaukee, have been doing projects in conjunction with the Boston-based Institute for Healthcare Improvement. And, he says, that previous work "and the commitment to quality improvement have made further integration easier."

St. Joseph's as a Learning Lab

A significant portion of the serious foundational work for this system-wide wave of change began at Wheaton Franciscan-St. Joseph, when, back in 2002, Wisconsin's quality improvement organization (QIO), MetaStar, contacted St. Joseph's CEO and then-chief nursing officer, says Barbara Rogness, RN, director of quality for Wheaton Franciscan Healthcare-St. Joseph. "The QIO was looking to partner with a hospital in the state, and thought that St. Joseph's would be a good hospital to partner with," she recalls. MetaStar also sponsored the participation of clinician leaders from St. Joseph in conferences of the Boston-based Institute for Healthcare Improvement.

The initial focus of the program that Wheaton Franciscan-St. Joseph was involved in with MetaStar was surgical infections. And within a very short period of time, as part of the Surgical Site Infection Prevention (SIP) project, the St. Joseph's team had decreased the infection rate in cardiac surgeries by 71%, in caesarean sections by 100%, in colorectal surgeries by 100%, and in vascular surgeries by 65%. (The SIP project involved more than 50 hospitals nationwide and was coordinated by the Seattle-based QIO Qualis Health.)

Fresh off this initial surgical infection improvement work, the clinicians at St. Joseph's kept moving forward, turning their attention to a variety of different areas for improvement, all under the broad objective of bringing down mortality rates. As a result, Rogness notes, "Within a two-year period of focusing efforts to decrease mortality, Wheaton Franciscan Healthcare-St. Joseph had experienced a 35% decrease in its raw mortality rate. By 2005, the hospital's rate had decreased to below the national average in the Hospital Standardized Mortality Rate, per Institute for Healthcare Improvement data."

Glucose Monitoring: In-the-Trenches Work

Another area that the team at Wheaton Franciscan-St. Joseph took on is typical of the challenging, in-the-trenches kind of quality improvement work that pioneering hospital organizations are engaging in these days, despite the fact that such work requires sustained commitment and energy over long periods of time in order to yield significant results. And that is in blood glucose monitoring of post-operative inpatients.

"We started in 2002, and are still working on it," Rogness reports. The glucose monitoring initiative emerged out of an optional quality measure that some hospitals in the IHI collaborative were working on. "At the time," Rogness recalls, "the literature was indicating that you would want to control glucose in your post-operative patients, especially in cardiac patients. At that time, the goal was to keep a patient's serum glucose level under 200—that was what the literature was indicating. And we found that our post-surgical patients were tending to be above 200."

The core clinical challenge, Rogness notes, is the complexity involved in addressing all the variables that could account for high glucose levels in post-operative patients. On the heels of work already initiated in the surgical infection program, Rogness and her colleagues initially limited their efforts to control post-operative patients' glucose levels to post-cardiac surgery patients. "But," she says, "we very quickly realized that, scientifically, your body doesn't know if you've had heart or knee surgery; so it didn't make a lot of sense to stay limited to the cardiac surgery patients." So the program has grown to encompass all inpatients. Among the challenges: addressing the differing aspects of care for type 1 and for type 2 diabetics; developing a multidisciplinary approach and commitment to this area; and making the practical leap to translating the guidelines implied in the general clinical literature into specific care steps.

"It's a real cultural change to get people to realize you don't need a diagnosis of diabetes to look at that and treat it," Rogness says. "And that was a huge change for nurses. In the past," she adds, "we were more worried about a reading of 80, or hypoglycemia; and we've really had to change the attitude of the nursing staff to recognize that a reading of 200 is more harmful than one of 80."

How has work in this area become successful over time? The Wheaton Franciscan-St. Joseph clinician leaders hired an advanced practice nurse who was certified in diabetes to do glucose management for the hospital's patients. That nurse also coordinates carefully with two nurses in the ICU in order to do the management in that unit. A daily glucose rounding process was established; initially, it was led by an intensivist, but that model was modified, so that, currently, the APN and the medical director of the ICU are leading those rounds. Ultimately, once the hospital's intensivist staffing shortage is addressed, the program will revert to an intensivist-led model. Importantly, the multidisciplinary rounding involves not only the nurse directly caring for each patient, but also a representative from nutrition, physical therapy, respiratory therapy, a case manager, sometimes the charge nurse on duty, and either the coordinating APN or the ICU medical director. As part of the program, all ICU patients receive two glucose checks, and if a patient's glucose level is found to be above the set range, the hospital's glucose management protocol is automatically triggered. In addition, all patients coming into the hospital's ICU or PACU are now given a finger-stick test for glucose, in order to determine their glucose level as early as possible.

Work is ongoing at Wheaton Franciscan-St. Joseph with regard to the evolution of the glucose management program. What's important to note, Rogness says, is that the glucose management effort is one element in a very broad range of efforts all moving forward at St. Joseph's, and increasingly, across Wheaton Franciscan Healthcare. Rapid response teams have been developed in more than one area at St. Joseph's, and the hospital also has ventilator-associated pneumonia and central-line infection programs underway.

For the nurses who are so involved in such at-the-bedside issues in patient care, the growth and evolution of a nursing shared governance process through the hospital's Shared Governance Council has been critical to nursing buy-in for change, Rogness notes. In addition, the work of that council is linked to the work of the hospital's Shared Governance Quality Council, she adds.

"One of the things we do on a monthly basis," Rogness reports, "is that three or four of the departments bring to us what they're doing in terms of quality improvement. And it's so empowering and revitalizing to hear what the staff nurses are doing in their area to improve care and outcomes—there are unbelievable and remarkable stories. So we really have created a culture where the staff know that this is part of their job here and professionally." Inevitably, there is at least one "naysayer" in any group of clinicians, she says; but, she quickly adds, "If I can get that person on board, the culture on that whole unit will change. And that can make a huge difference in your outcomes."

On the physician side of the process of cultural change, Cardamone says that "It sounds cliché, but physicians need to be involved early and often," in order to spur the kind of changes in an organization's physician culture that will support quality transformation. "There's often this feeling that everything has to be wrapped up and ready to present first," he observes, "but it's very difficult to get physician participation that way." The two other critical elements in achieving physician buy-in when it comes to engaging in transformative quality work, he says, are the ability to achieve a "consensus about the patient being at the center" of all change-based efforts; and "the availability of timely and actionable data for physicians to help them to really be a catalyst for continuous improvement and learning."

What's more, Cardamone says, "The ability to engage folks in a multi-disciplinary way" is essential to creating a culture of change and quality transformation. "The clinical evidence is really a foundation for improvement; the engagement of all disciplines is important; and," he says, "there is an additional factor, what I call the 'leave-your-egos-at-the-door' element, which means making sure that everyone has a say in things without regard to an individual's position or role. A tremendous respect for what everyone does is now hardwired into the culture at St. Joe's," he says. The development of a strong partnership between physicians and hospital administrators is critical. "If you have your chief of your medical staff, all your physician leaders, and your hospital president, all articulating and professing the same message of quality improvement and concern for patient care, that approach will really help drive cultural change as it has at St. Joe's." Finally, he says, "Our faith-based heritage is important. It doesn't matter that we're Catholic, but our respect for integrity and ethics really speaks to our larger health care ministry in the organization. And that isn't just a set of words on the wall, it really calls people to work in this organization, as opposed to in others."

On a practical level, Rogness says, it comes down to relationships. "We've shared our story with a lot of people," she says, "and I'm often asked how we got physicians and nurses to collaborate together. There are a number of ways we've done it, but there is nothing more important than the relationships you have." Part of the key there has been actively cultivating physician champions who will spread the gospel of quality-targeted change, she says. This is true in every specific area of endeavor, as well as generally. For example, she and her colleagues in the quality improvement area quickly got an endocrinologist on board to help champion the glucose management effort at a very early stage. This is something doable at any hospital-based organization, she says. It's a matter of "looking to relationships on the floor and on the unit" on which to base collaborative partnerships early on.

Automation and Transparency Commitments Included

All this talk of partnership is backed up by some practical investments, especially with regard to information technology. As the Wheaton Franciscan system's 2007 annual report states, "A major facet of our Clinical Performance Excellence initiative is implementation of our Electronic Health Record (EHR). Year one of the three-year, $61 million EHR project has been completed on schedule," the report notes. "When fully implemented, the EHR promises to significantly enhance quality of patient care as well as the practice environment for physicians and other clinicians." Indeed, the report goes on to note that "As physician involvement is integral to the success of the EHR, physician engagement has been a key priority in this initial phase." And it goes on to quote Patrick Spiering, MD, of the Wheaton Franciscan Medical Group, who notes that "The main area of improvement for physicians is the ability to access medical records throughout the system remotely; for example, when you're on call at home in the middle of the night."

Transparency is another element in all this. Cardamone notes that "In Wisconsin, we participate in the Wisconsin Collaborative for Health Care Quality. It's a voluntary organization designed to promote quality and transparency through the publication of clinical quality data, and it's a model for organizations around the country."

As a result of all the work being done to transform quality of care in the system, Wheaton Franciscan in 2007 was ranked at or above the 90th percentile nationally in key clinical quality measures for patients with congestive heart failure, pneumonia, and acute myocardial infarction (heart attack) according to the methodology used in the Hospital Quality Incentive Demonstration Project (HQID) cosponsored by the Centers for Medicare and Medicaid Services (CMS) and Premier Inc.

Going forward, leaders at Wheaton Franciscan say they want to continue to ramp up their quality work, spread it across the entire system, and then assess gains made so far and concentrate on the most impactful efforts possible. "I think we'll continue to see this escalation of work for a period of time, but there will also be the recognition that there will need to be a focus on what the most important efforts are, because there are resource issues, so we'll focus on what's most important in adding value," says Cardamone, who adds that that will be true both at Wheaton Franciscan and among quality pioneer organizations in general in the next few years, as clear gains are made in transformative quality work.

At the same time, Cardamone says, demands for documented quality and for transparency of both quality and outcomes-related information will only continue to accelerate on the part of purchasers, payers, and consumers. Pay-for-performance initiatives, broader outcomes reporting efforts more generally, and external pressures to improve quality are simply going to be a part of the landscape for providers going forward. "So," he says, "trying to balance priorities, making improvements in many areas, and adequately resourcing those areas" will be challenges for everyone. "And it's not a static environment," he adds. "But that's what makes it very exciting."

8

Change Facilitator: Information Technology and the Pursuit of Quality Transformation

There is a strong paradox embedded in the inter-relationship between transformative quality work and information technology (IT) implementation. On the one hand, there is a clear consensus among clinician and executive leaders in health care quality that simply automating the flawed patient care and clinician workflow processes that exist in hospital organizations across the United States and internationally is no solution at all. Indeed, as numerous patient care organizations have already discovered, doing so can make things worse, in two ways: First, when the leaders of an organization pursue flawed automation strategies without first reinventing or reworking care processes, they waste precious time and human and financial resources that ultimately are ill-spent. Second, flawed automation can actually augment resistance to change, by convincing reluctant clinicians and others in an organization that moving forward to change processes will only bring problems and pain.

That having been said, there is no question that the small minority of hospitals and health systems that can be said to be pioneers in the quality revolution are without exception also innovating very aggressively to implement transformation-facilitative information technology. As demonstrated by the case studies in subsequent chapters, when information technology is applied intelligently, strategically, and planfully, it truly becomes a facilitator to vastly improved quality, patient safety, and transparency in patient care organizations.

In short, information technology alone is never a panacea, and can actually become a hindrance to quality transformation if poorly implemented. But when linked strategically to the highest-level quality, patient safety, and transparency goals of any patient care organization, IT can be a co-agent of transformation.

What's more, once one begins to look at some of the most critical quality, patient safety and transparency innovations that purchasers, payers and, increasingly, consumers, are demanding that providers make in health care, none are achievable without considerable IT support. Even a tiny sample of the imperatives facing patient care organizations demonstrates the essential facilitative role of IT:

- Standardization of care processes, organization-wide
- Elimination of medical errors, organization-wide
- True closed-loop medication management for dramatic reduction in medication errors
- Development and use of standardized physician order sets
- Universalization of availability of all relevant patient information at the point of care, out as far as the physician office and home, and across all relevant outpatient sites, via Web enablement
- Clinical decision support for physicians and nurses at the point of care
- Optimized documentation by clinicians into the patient record
- Development of true closed-loop medication management and administration, with systems linked to optimize medication processes for all clinicians and eliminate or reduce medication errors
- Facilitation of disease management across the spectrum of care
- Data analysis for quality performance improvement
- Data analysis for optimizing clinician workflow
- Facilitation of the availability of diagnostic images by all appropriate clinicians
- Collection of outcomes data for publication in pay-for-performance and other programs
- Use of data to motivate individual clinicians to improve outcomes
- Application of performance improvement methodologies to problems throughout an organization
- Creation of transparency of clinical outcomes for stakeholder groups in the community
- Participation in personal health record programs for consumers/ patients

AND THE LIST GOES ON

Those organizational leaders who know the true value of information technology are using IT strategically to enable vast change initiatives in their organizations. One good example is Northwestern Memorial Hospital in Chicago. The 897-bed academic medical center has spent well over $100 million implementing core clinical information systems alone, including its electronic medical record (EMR) and computerized physician order entry (CPOE) systems. At Northwestern Memorial (see case study, pages 74–82), as at other quality pioneer organizations discussed in this book, IT is never a value in itself, but rather a nuts-and-bolts facilitator of broad and intensive quality work.

Tim Zoph, Northwestern Memorial's vice-president and chief information officer (CIO), puts it this way: "IT in and of itself as a discipline is not a singular pathway for advancing quality," Zoph says. "Our experience here has been around creating a culture of safety and of process improvement and quality, and having IT being an enabler and facilitator, and an accelerator. We were able to evolve our quality, safety, and technology in parallel. In some ways, technology also provides the infrastructure for improvement. We're really starting to get the leverage from that technology now that we have the culture, and the full adoption of the technology. It's important to know how and where to look for the benefits as our industry is only at the very beginning stage of technology adoption for quality. The value is yet to come, and the way to drive the value is through disciplined improvement in your environment. And we count our projects in the hundreds. But it's an institutional discipline and culture; that's the value."

Not only is Zoph one of the industry's visionaries with regard to the strategic use of IT to promote change in patient care; he is also a prime example of the emergence of the truly strategic CIO, a hospital or health system executive who spends his days helping others in the executive suite and members of his organization's board translate objectives for revolutions in quality, efficiency, and transparency into concrete plans for creating IT-facilitated paths towards those goals.

Executives like Zoph are collaborating with clinician and non-clinician leaders in their organizations to use IT strategically to move forward on a vast array of initiatives to improve care quality, safety, and transparency. Consider the following:

- The Novi, Michigan-based Trinity Health, the nation's fourth-largest Catholic health system, continues to move forward with ongoing work towards what it describes as the nation's largest community-based hospital health care IT initiative, encompassing 31 hospitals across seven states (Maryland, Ohio, Michigan, Indiana, Iowa, Idaho, and California). To date, the Trinity Health organization has spent over $315 million on its initiative, dubbed Project Genesis, whose aim is to leverage massive gains in quality and safety through the facilitative use of IT tools, including system-wide EMR and CPOE systems. Among other things, clinical IT is being used at Trinity Health to facilitate in the development and use of standardized, evidence-based order sets in a number of clinical areas; in the development of standardized clinical process workflows in a number of areas; in the use of a standardized approach to the measurement and evaluation of pain in post-hip and -knee replacement patients (see full case study on Trinity Health, pp. 86–95).

- Clinician and IT leaders at Brigham and Women's Hospital in Boston have developed a comprehensive database that includes all patient safety incident report data, and that produces quarterly reports highlighting patient safety trends by severity, item, and frequency, for all relevant clinicians and managers in the organization, and that helps clinicians and managers evaluate the organization's ongoing journey towards transformative quality and patient safety (see full case study on Brigham and Women's Hospital, pp. 44–53).

- Children's Hospital of Wisconsin, in Milwaukee, in June 2000 became the first pediatric hospital in the United States to go live with CPOE, according to Carl G. M. Weigle, MD, the 236-bed hospital's medical director of information services. Since then, voluntary reports of medication errors have gone up by 4.25% (indicating that more errors are being caught than was previously possible), while incident reports related to medication orders have gone down by 5.53%, and incident reports related to lab tests have gone down by 4.02%, Weigle reports. More broadly, he says, CPOE implementation has been a facilitator of the drive to create a culture of quality and safety across the organization.

- At the seven-hospital OSF Healthcare in Peoria, Illinois, patient safety officer John Whittington, MD, reports that, in the past couple of years, using Six Sigma techniques, "We've done a lot of work on hospital-acquired pressure ulcers, and have driven down our rates to 3%, from much higher rates—that's world-class." In another example, the system has aggressively attacked the universal problem of ventilator-associated pneumonia. Using Six Sigma techniques, the system has reduced the rate of such pneumonia by 400%, from a rate of approximately 4 incidents per 1,000 ventilator days, to about 1 per 1,000 ventilator days. At the flagship OSF-St. Francis Hospital, some individual units have been able to go for whole months without a single incident, he adds.

- At the 366-bed Decatur Memorial Hospital in Decatur, Illinois, Linda Fahey, RN, vice-president and chief nurse executive, notes that her organization turned to the Six Sigma methodology for answers after the hospital's CEO learned of the impressive strides that the Lafayette, Indiana-based Caterpillar construction and agricultural equipment company, which operates a plant in Decatur, had made using that process. Using Six Sigma techniques, Fahey and her clinician colleagues were able to strongly improve the availability of routine medications, from 78.6% availability to 86% availability, and to improve medication delivery from 109 minutes to 21 minutes, for routine medications available in the medication dispensing cabinets on patient care floors.

- Decades of self-development of clinical information systems at Intermountain Healthcare in Salt Lake City have led to one of the most longstanding clinical decision support systems in the country. "We wouldn't have built the infrastructure we did, if decision support hadn't been the focus," says Peter Haug, MD, director of the Homer Warner Center for Informatics Research and a senior informaticist for the integrated delivery system. The key innovation that took place at Intermountain decades ago, he says, was a focus on clinical decision support and on support of clinicians in general, rather than on billing functions, as was the norm in early IS development. As a result he says, Intermountain's leaders have created a system that is supporting a wealth of clinical outcomes reporting, data analysis, and clinical care improvement, and has won the organization numerous awards.

NOT JUST THE MECHANICAL ASPECTS: THE PARADOX OF CPOE

The paradox that leaders of health care organizations who are using IT strategically recognize is this: Without IT, quality transformation is ultimately not possible—certainly not organization-wide. Yet IT implementation must be done with foresight, intelligence, and a great deal of thought planning in order to leverage the technology as a change facilitator.

A perfect example of this is the implementation of CPOE systems. On their own, CPOE systems are no panacea. In fact, asking physicians to electronically enter their orders simply to improve efficiency, without providing them with the host of benefits implicit in the technology, is asking for trouble, as the executives at Cedars-Sinai Medical Center famously learned when they mandated CPOE use by their doctors in 2002. The "Cedars CPOE debacle" became symbolic for many in the industry of clinical IT implementations gone bad, and probably caused some CEOs and CIOs to become unnecessarily "gun-shy" about CPOE implementation. As *CIO Magazine* put it in a June 2003 article:

> [O]nly 3 to 5% of American hospitals have fully implemented CPOE systems. What gives? Clues to this puzzle can be found in the disaster that recently befell a new CPOE implementation at Cedars-Sinai Medical Center in Los Angeles. As the Cedars-Sinai story illustrates, there is a right way to install CPOE systems and a wrong way. The teaching hospital, some observers say, took the latter approach—a Big Bang adoption that required all of its physicians to show they could use the new system on one day or lose their privileges to admit patients. Three months later, hundreds of Cedars-Sinai physicians revolted, voting to suspend their usage of the hospital's CPOE system indefinitely.[1]

As attendees at health care conferences in 2002, 2003, and beyond know, the "Cedars-Sinai debacle" became an iconic sort of cautionary tale for the industry. Unfortunately, the retelling of the story probably also inhibited some organizations from moving forward on clinical IT with the necessary alacrity, at least for a few years.

Yet what clinician and executive leaders at the boldest, most pioneering hospital-based organizations have learned is this: Effective CPOE implementation, which can result in tremendous reductions in medication and other medical errors, can hugely improve the efficiency of physicians, nurses, pharmacists, and techs of all kinds in hospitals, and can help cement a culture of quality in an organization—relies on very extensive foundational work in putting into place the EMR, a pharmacy system, an electronic medication administration record (eMAR) system, and all the connective interfaces or links, first, before going live with CPOE. Thus, successful CPOE implementations are the crowning glory of intensive and extensive clinical IT development in hospital-based organizations, not a tentative first step. As a result, only a very small percentage of hospitals have put the full range of systems in place—and are thus positioned to reap the enormous benefits of automation with regard to improved care quality, patient safety, and efficiency/clinician workflow optimization.

WHAT HAPPENS AT ADVANCED IT IMPLEMENTATION STAGES

Dave Garets, one of the people in the health care industry who has studied this question the most extensively, sees CPOE implementation as one of the very last phases in a broad clinical IT implementation pathway, with seven stages, the seventh being the ultimate level, and one that naturally no U.S. patient care organization has yet attained.

Garets, president and CEO of HIMSS Analytics, a division of the Chicago-based Healthcare Information and Management Systems Society (HIMSS), and his colleague, executive vice-president Michael W. Davis, in 2007 developed a seven-stage EMR adoption model (see Figure 8.1 and Figure 8.2) that they use in order to interpret and categorize hospital-based organizations' progress towards full adoption of the core suite of clinical information systems needed to move hospitals and health systems to full use of the tools needed to make progress on efficiency, quality, and safety.

EMR Adoption Model		
Stage	Cumulative Capabilities	% of Hospitals
Stage 7	Medical record fully electronic; CDO able to contribute to ICEHR as byproduct of SEHR	0.0%
Stage 6	Physician documentation (structured templates), full CDSS (variance & compliance), full PACS	0.1%
Stage 5	Closed loop medication administration	0.5%
Stage 4	CPOE, CDSS (clinical protocols)	3.0%
Stage 3	Clinical documentation (flow sheets), CDSS (error checking), PACS available outside Radiology	18.0%
Stage 2	CDR, CMV, CDSS inference engine, may have Document Imaging	38.8%
Stage 1	Ancillaries – Lab, Rad, Pharmacy	18.9%
Stage 0	All three Ancillaries not installed	20.7%

FIGURE 8.1. SOURCE: HIMSS ANALYTICS, 2007.[2]

Stage	Description
0	• Some clinical automation may exist. • Laboratory and/or pharmacy and/or radiology not installed.
1	• All three major ancillaries (laboratory, pharmacy and radiology) installed.
2	• Major ancillary clinical systems feed data to clinical data repository (CDR) that provides physician access for retrieving and reviewing results. • CDR contains a controlled medical vocabulary (CMV) and the clinical decision support system and rules engine for rudimentary conflict checking. • *Optional for extra points* - Information from document imaging systems may be linked to the CDR.
3	• Clinical documentation installed (e.g. vital signs, flow sheets, nursing notes, care plan charting, and/or the electronic medication administration record (eMAR) system are scored with extra points and are implemented and integrated with the CDR for at least one service in the hospital. • First level of clinician decision support is implemented to conduct error checking with order entry (i.e. drug/drug, drug/food, drug/lab, conflict checking normally found in the pharmacy). • Some level of medical image access from picture archive and communication systems (PACS) is available for access by physicians via the organization's intranet or other secure networks.
4	• Computerized practitioner/physician order entry (CPOE) for use by any clinician added to nursing and CDR environment. • Second-level of clinical decision support related to evidence-based medicine protocols implemented. • If one patient service area has implemented CPOE and completed previous stages, this stage has been achieved.
5	• The closed loop medication administration environment is fully implemented in at least one patient care service area. The eMAR and bar coding or other auto-identification technology, such as radio frequency identification (RRD), are implemented and integrated with CPOE and pharmacy to maximize point-of-care patient safety processes for medication administration.
6	• Full physician documentation/charting (structured templates) are implemented in at least one patient care service area. • A full complement of radiology PACS systems is implemented (i.e. all images, both digital and firm-based, are available to physicians via an intranet or other secure network.
7	• Clinical information can be readily shared via electronic transaction or exchange of electronic records with all entities within a regional health network (i.e., other hospitals, ambulatory clinics, sub-acute environments, employers, payers and patients).

FIGURE 8.2. SOURCE: HIMSS ANALYTICS, 2007.[2]

As of early 2008, Garets and Davis had determined that, by their exacting yardstick, approximately 25 non-Veterans Administration hospitals in the United States had reached Stage 6 of the EMR adoption model.

What did those hospitals get for their investment of money, time, human resources, and effort? In a 2007 report for HIMSS Analytics, Davis wrote that "Hospitals that have achieved Stage 6 of the EMRAM [EMR Adoption Model] have made significant executive commitments and investments to reach this stage. Once achieved, Stage 6 hospitals appear to have a significant advantage over competitors for patient safety, clinician support, clinician recruitment, and competitive marketing for both consumers and nurse recruitment. Most of the Stage 6 hospitals have almost fully automated/paperless medical records, and are either starting to evaluate their data for care delivery process improvements, or are already documenting significant improvements in this area."

Further, Davis wrote in the 2007 report, "While the investments to achieve Stage 6 of the EMRAM are not insignificant, they are within reach of most hospitals. Once achieved, the IT capital budgets decline, while the IT staffing and IT operating budgets in many cases increase to support the more sophisticated clinical capabilities—but not to the total IT budget level that was in place during the implementation of the more complex EMRAM stages (e.g., Stages 3–6)."

Among the "significant improvements in care delivery and in operational efficiency" that Stage 6 hospitals have achieved include the following (according to the HIMSS Analytics report):

- The uncovering of more medication errors, but also significant reductions in medication errors. "In one case," Davis's report notes, "a hospital has prevented 170 wrong patient errors; 1,500 wrong drug errors; 203 wrong dose errors; 2,947 wrong time errors; and 26 wrong route errors out of 158,684 administered doses. Another facility reports that 42% of errors attributed to handwriting have been eliminated, and omitted drugs have been reduced by 70%."
- A reduction in elapsed time from medication orders to medication dispensing of 15 to 20 minutes for routine orders, and less that 10 minutes for STAT orders.
- Diagnostic report turnaround times gauged in minutes rather than hours.
- Reduction in nursing overtime (one hospital reported $3,000,000 annual savings in that area), in the use of agency nurses (another hospital reported the elimination of $2 million in agency nursing costs), improvements in physician and nurse recruitment, and

reductions in claims denials (one facility reported coding denials dropping from 9.2 to 2.2%).

Garets and Davis have been adhering to their highly rigorous model, and do not consider hospital organizations that have not implemented all the elements of each phase to have reached the subsequent phase in their model. As a result, a number of hospital organizations nationwide that have achieved some of the attainments in Stages 4, 5, and 6 of the HIMSS Analytics model, but not all, would not be considered by HIMSS Analytics to have reached those overall levels of development.

HIMSS LEADERSHIP SURVEY REVEALS INDUSTRY-WIDE PUSH TOWARDS CLINICAL IT FACILITATION

While the vast majority of U.S. hospitals are still in very early stages of clinical IT development, as measured by HIMSS Analytics, the broader HIMSS organization's 2008 annual survey results show just how important hospital organization executives now realize such development is, and why.[3] HIMSS Leadership Survey respondents, in a survey whose results were released at the annual HIMSS Conference on February 28, 2008 in Orlando, Florida, said that their top five IT priorities were as follows: replacing/upgrading/ implementing clinical information systems (40%); implementing technology to reduce medical errors/promote patient safety (39%); implementing an EMR or its components (38%); connecting hospital IT with remote environments such as physicians' offices and homes (30%); and using IT for business continuity and disaster recovery (27%).

Asked what application areas they considered most important over the course of the next two years, HIMSS Survey respondents pointed to clinical information systems (45%), CPOE (42%), EMR (31%), enterprise-wide clinical information sharing (30%), closed-loop medication management (30%), clinical data repository (29%), point-of-care data collection (21%), and clinical portals (21%). In other words, all top eight application priorities mentioned by survey respondents were clinical.

Once CPOE is achieved, important things happen. As Carl G. M. Weigle, MD, medical director of information services at the 236-bed Children's Hospital of Wisconsin, in Milwaukee, notes, CPOE becomes a part of the broader effort to transform quality and safety in a hospital organization. "One of the biggest things to happen for us has been the recognition that CPOE implementation by itself is really just laying down a safety infrastructure," Weigle says. "You can put alerts in and force people to follow certain procedures; but until you create an integration of the order entry system with pharmacy, or at least a two-way interface, and some automation of medication administration documentation using barcoding or RFID—you have to tie those things all together in a loop, and we're working on that—that's where the big advances take place." Weigle confirms that enterprise-wide barcoded medication administration has been in place since June 2007 at Children's.

Use of CPOE has been closely linked to several patient safety initiatives at Children's, Weigle notes. One sentinel event with regard to blood products spurred the use of CPOE to improve safety in that area. "We think that the ordering, preparation and administering blood products in the hospital is an incredibly risky process," he says. "We did an FMEA process on it three or four years ago," he reports, referring to the failure mode and effects analysis analytic procedure. What came out of it, he reports, is the reworking of the ordering of blood products to greatly enhance patient safety; and with the use of CPOE as a required gateway to doing such ordering.

CHICKEN OR EGG?

"Information technology will play a critical role in enabling new processes that respond to the Four Truths," says a recent report from First Consulting Group (now a part of the Falls Church, Virginia-based CSC Corporation), referring to four statements FCG researchers say will be true of the emerging health care system. (These include high expectations for the safety of patient care; increased cost pressures on patient care organizations to become more efficient; that the care experience will have to become more patient-centered; and that payers and consumers will demand quality and cost transparency). "Process improvement alone goes only so far without the assistance of IT," the 2008 report states. "IT absent a conscious effort to optimize process will only perpetuate what's in place today. Organizations that do the best job of reaching a new level of organizational excellence will combine both elements. To be successful, they will need to become excellent in all of the dimensions suggested by the four truths: safety, efficiency, patient-centeredness, and accountability/transparency."

Erica Drazen, ScD, a partner in the Emerging Practices division at CSC Corporation and one of the three authors of the report (along with FCG/CSC colleagues Jane Metzger and Jason Fortin), says with regard to the findings in her group's report that "Hospital organizations will need to have data for accountability, and to understand what practices are going on in institutions. Most hospital organizations," she says, "have committees of the board that worry about this; but without a standard practice, it's really hard to see how you're doing. Clearly, whenever they're looking at one of these new mandates or initiatives [for quality reporting], they need to look at the solution through an IT lens, because it takes so many resources. They might have a core documentation element of the EMR, but the data may not be organized or coded." The result, she notes, is that large numbers of hospital organizations, in order to satisfy increasing demands for quality transparency, are doing data analysis on paper, using teams of nurses and other staff members to fulfill the data demands from various programs and organizations. That, she says flatly, "is crazy."

Along the way, Drazen continues, "CPOE will be a key facilitator. Right now," she says, "CPOE is a key motivator for things that need to be done anyway, such as standard order sets. The order set should vary based on the patient; right now, it varies based on the provider, which makes no sense at all. There's no reason that Dr. Smith's patients should need something different from Dr. Jones's patients, though you and I might need different care." Thus, moving forward on standardizing order sets, she says, is a clear imperative for hospital organizations, and is linked closely to CPOE as a foundation for CPOE implementation. Yet very few community hospitals in particular, she says, have done such foundational work in order to be able to move forward with CPOE. In other words, there remain a large number of chicken-or-egg types of issues going forward in hospital organizations as their leaders look to IT to help facilitate change, but find that they need to facilitate IT first.

Drazen and her colleagues estimate CPOE and EMR adoption a bit differently from how the HIMSS Analytics folks do it. According to CSC, approximately 10% of U.S. hospitals have live CPOE, 20% have implemented eMAR, and about 8% have gone live with both technologies.

TOWARDS "CLINICAL INTELLIGENCE"

With a galaxy of possible uses to which hospital organizations can intelligently apply information technology, how can hospital leaders create sets of priorities to aspire to? Obviously, they must look to the broadest quality, safety, transparency, and business goals of their organizations when considering how to use IT strategically.

One important concept to consider is what Drazen and her colleagues at FCG/CSC are terming "clinical intelligence." If any concept articulated an advanced state of thinking and application, it would be this one. "The real value of IT comes when you can analyze systems and proactively change patient care processes," says Fran Turisco, research expert in the Emerging Practices division at FCG-now-CSC. "CSC calls it 'health informatics,' we call it 'clinical intelligence,' but it's the same thing," Turisco explains. It means making changes farther upstream to improve care quality and safety. "Pay for performance reporting and clinical quality measures are only the first step. That kind of reporting is like checking a box to comply with data mandates from CMS, JCAHO, or other organizations. But the real value comes when you can move upstream and become proactive. For example, making sure that we give patients presenting with pneumonia antibiotics within the first four hours. Or the QA department gets a list of patients at high risk for various clinical conditions, like those on warfarin or who come in with pneumonia, and they automatically get logged into an application that monitors their care." And of course, data is continually used to analyze and improve care patterns.

Turisco says she and her colleagues envision "a multi-pronged approach where you could bake clinical alerts into your system, so it would tell you things such as, you have to give this medication within four hours, and now you're in hour three. Or it would alert you that some patients are not at the level they should be. For example, if you're noticing that a patient's lab values are changing, and a medication is needed, or you need physician intervention. In those cases, you need to build intelligence into it, so the system identifies what needs to be done."

Such applications remain futuristic for the vast majority of patient care organizations, but perhaps not for long, Turisco says. Indeed, she believes many commercial clinical IT vendors will be able to offer such capabilities within five years.

HEIGHTENED EXPECTATIONS

It is very important to keep in mind that, as pioneering organizations demonstrate the value of clinical IT as a facilitator of improved care quality, patient safety, clinician workflow, transparency, and other values, early successes will only raise expectations for the value of IT industry-wide, among all stakeholder groups (including purchasers, payers, and consumers, not to mention clinicians). "We're looking at an evolving industry. There are higher expectations and more expectations than in the past," Claudia Tessier, vice-president of the Medical Records Institute, recently told the magazine *Future Healthcare* in an interview regarding the Medical Records Institute's annual Survey of Electronic Medical Records Trends and Usage.[4] As a result, Tessier told *Future Healthcare*, the results found in her organization's survey continue to change over time. "We found that the top five factors cited by more than 50% of the respondents working in hospitals are: patient safety, efficiency and convenience, satisfaction of physicians, the need to survive, and creating a medical community. Patient safety and creating a medical community are options that were not even offered in the past," she told the magazine.

Meanwhile, the Medical Record Institute's Ninth Annual Survey (of 819 EMR "decision-makers" and "influencers") found in 2007 that:

- The two most cited priorities for strategic decisions in IT were "the need to improve clinical processes or workflow efficiency," and "the need to improve quality of care."
- The three factors most cited as driving the need for EMR systems in hospitals were "patient safety considerations," "efficiency and convenience," and "satisfaction of physicians and clinician employees."
- The three factors cited most often as driving the need for EMRs in the physician environment were "improved patient documentation," "efficiency and convenience to physicians through workflow benefits," and "remote access to patient information."
- Meanwhile, the barriers most often cited by survey respondents to EMR implementation were "lack of adequate funding or resources," "anticipated difficulties in changing to an EMR system," "difficulty in creating a migration plan from paper to electronic documentation and recordkeeping," and "inability to find an EMR solution or components at an affordable cost."[5]

All the factors cited above for the various priorities, implementation drivers, and barriers are actually quite thoroughly related, both positively and negatively. We know, for instance, that clinicians will make use of clinical IT if it supports their daily workflow, and, yes, convenience. Conversely, they will resist, as the Cedars-Sinai attendings did, IT that does not help them and that is felt to be a hindrance.

Yet when they are provided tools that help them and are clearly of benefit to them and to their patients, physicians, nurses, pharmacists, and other clinicians can become fierce champions of both IT adoption and of the process and quality change it helps to facilitate.

A MAJOR FRONTIER—THE SHIFT TOWARDS OUTPATIENT

There is also the imperative for hospital organizations to expand their IT reach to encompass the outpatient sphere; and for physician groups to move forward on their own as well. Lyle Berkowitz, MD, a practicing internal medicine physician who is the medical director of clinical information systems for the Northwestern Memorial Physicians Group (NMPG), the 100-physician primary care affiliate group of Northwestern Memorial Hospital in Chicago, is involved in just such efforts. As an affiliate of the hospital, NMPG is working closely with hospital IT leaders to devise and implement solutions that work for NMPG's office-based physicians but also make sense for Northwestern Memorial Hospital.

In fact, NMPG physicians are fortunate in having an outpatient EMR that fully communicates with the hospital's inpatient EMR, and in fact is an integrated product from a single vendor. As a practicing internal medicine specialist, Berkowitz says the potential for revolutionizing care quality and clinician workflow across the inpatient and outpatient sphere is tremendous. Still, he says, "The major strategic issue to recognize is that a single EMR for both inpatient and outpatient has both pros and cons. The major 'pro': access to information across the enterprise, with the caveat that you need both a strategic and tactical initiative to make sure all the right people know about the data in the system. The 'con'? Information overload. From an outpatient perspective, I don't need all the data from the inpatient encounter. We've been able to balance this by customizing our default view in two ways," he adds. "First, we filter which information we see in our default notes, removing certain inpatient notes that don't have significant relevance to us, such as pastoral notes and nursing notes; and we compress the time interval to allow only one column of data per day. So we see just one column of inpatient data, rather than 12."

In other words, in the outpatient sphere as much as in the inpatient sphere, it's all about providing clinicians with the information they need at the point of care, for effective diagnosing, prescribing, treatment, referral, and communication—but not overloading them or marring their workflow.

Once again, Berkowitz's position is consonant with that of clinicians and clinician executives across the health care system, and that is, essentially, this: make the clinicians' work lives better and easier, help them to more optimally treat patients, and to participate in quality-driven change—but don't hinder them from their moment-to-moment work with patients or with data.

CONCLUSION

As can be seen from the text of this chapter, there is a paradox built into the issues around information technology and quality/patient safety/efficacy. Used strategically, IT can be exceptionally powerful in facilitating change. But by itself, it is simply a tool like any other. Culture, process change, and all the foundational work needed to correctly implement clinical information systems, are all of enormous importance in ensuring their success after go-live.

Given those caveats regarding how the foundations for clinical IT must be laid in patient care organizations, the potential benefits are vast. To summarize, among the most important areas of potential include:

- Creating enterprise-wide patient record systems that allow all appropriate clinicians to have immediate access to the patient record and to use it fully and well at the point of care
- Providing clinical decision support, as relevant and appropriate, to all clinicians who need it at the point of care
- Integrating systems to facilitate such critical quality/patient safety goals as true closed-loop medication management and medication administration

- Using data to both document patient care, and then to analyze care patterns and feed data back into the quality transformation process
- Gathering data in order to support external data mandates, including pay-for-performance initiatives, outcomes measurement programs, and other efforts
- Using data, information and technology to support chronic care management
- Helping to foster such emerging concepts as the "medical home"
- Creating an ever-widening circle of appropriate clinical information availability. Thus, information-sharing will extend to outpatient sites inside and outside the enterprise, to physician use, and ultimately to consumers/patients, the community, and beyond (including to regional health information networks and the emergent national health information network)

Within the broader transformative quality journey of 1,000 miles, the facilitative IT journey can seem to be quite as long a distance to cover. But pioneering efforts from points across the U.S. health care system demonstrate that the journey is well and truly begun, and that the pace of efforts overall with regard to IT is accelerating, not as rapidly as some might hope, but far faster than many might have believed, as the health care system moves forward.

NOTES

1. Alison Bass, "Health-Care IT: A Big Rollout Bust," *CIO Magazine,* June 1, 2003. http://www.cio.com/article/29736/Health_Care_IT_A_Big_Rollout_Bust.
2. Mike Davis, "Stage 6 Hospitals: The Journey and the Accomplishments," HIMSS Analytics, 2007. http://www.google.com/search?hl=en&ie=ISO-8859-1&q=HIMS S+Analytics+Stage+6+hospitals.
3. "19th Annual 2008 HIMSS Leadership Survey." http://www.himss.org/2008Survey/ healthcareCIO_final.asp.
4. "EMR Systems: Separating the Wheat from the Chaff,": Interview with Claudia Tessier (no author cited). *Future Healthcare,* Q1 (2008): 91.
5. "Medical Records Institute's Ninth Annual Survey of Electronic Medical Records Trends and Usage 2007," Medical Records Institute. http://www.medrecinst.com/ MRI/emrsurvey.html. (accessed July 2008)

9

Working Conceptually: The Use of Performance Improvement Methodologies in Transformational Work

As can be seen in the case studies presented in this book (pp. 43–117), virtually all of the hospital organizations whose leaders have worked together to move their organizations forward to comprehensively transform care quality, patient safety, and transparency have made extensive use of performance improvement methodologies. Indeed, the emergence of the movement towards transformative quality has been concomitant with the broad rise in the use of such formal methodologies across health care.

This is no coincidence. As all those interviewed for this book agree, the challenge of remaking one's quality, patient safety, and transparency is no small task. Moving onto the quality journey perforce requires a sustained commitment to process work that is both broad and intensive. Also, much of the work is very complex and requires large teams of leaders and implementers with specialized knowledge.

Therefore, more hospitals and health systems are turning to formal performance methodologies in order to create and sustain major change.

In Chapter 1, business management avatar Peter Drucker has been quoted as saying that the U.S. health care system was the most complex industry he had ever tried to understand, bar none, and that large health care organizations may be the most complex developed in human history.[1]

If one accepts such an observation, it follows naturally that patient care organizations would need to use tools to manage the complexity of creating and sustaining change. Conversely, the fact that health care was until recently so late in adopting performance improvement methodology tools seems only to confirm how far behind our industry has been in comparison with other industries in terms of standardizing best practices and systematizing core production processes.

As I often stress in my presentations to audiences, there is a fact that must be kept in mind with regard to that slowness to standardize; and that is that health care has for many decades been an ever-growing, and now-gigantic, cottage industry. Paradoxically, one of the largest industries in the U.S. economy has never gone through a first "Industrial Revolution" of the type that created standardized processes in the manufacturing sector, and then in such important industries as retailing, financial services, and even the travel and hospitality industries. Now, health care is going through its Information Age revolution at the same time that organizational leaders are heroically attempting to standardize processes and eliminate unnecessary variation from core clinical processes. No wonder it all feels so difficult to so many!

Digging yet another level deeper, the question naturally arises as to why health care has until now never gone through a first "Industrial Revolution" of standardization of core production processes. There are a number of aspects to the answer; but the bottom-line short answer is that it has never had to. In other words, until recently, the employers who purchase health care services on behalf of their employees and employees' families, and the federal and state governments, have never demanded that health care providers standardize their processes. Part of this, of course, is that health care, uniquely among all the industries that produce services that are consumed in America, is overwhelmingly paid for by entities that are not the direct consumers of those services. What's more, the entities/individuals who primarily direct the expenditure of resources within producer organizations (patient care organizations in this case)—physicians—are for the most part not salaried employees of the organizations they work in (hospitals) and whose care they direct and provide. As is well known among industry experts, this produces a uniquely dramatic misalignment of incentives within the producer side of the health care economy. Indeed, the way in which physicians are positioned in the classic fee-for-service health care economy actually pits their interests at least partly against those of the hospitals in which they work, along a number of dimensions. For example, physicians make use of expensive diagnostic imaging services within hospitals, the operating costs of which fall on the hospitals, not on the doctors; yet these same doctors can, while working within hospitals, also legally develop freestanding imaging centers that compete for income with those hospitals. Were one to try to translate this kind of situation into any other industry, it simply could not be done.

Delving into the profound complexity of these misaligned incentives is obviously beyond the scope of this book. But one thing is important to note, and that is that because most physicians—the most powerful individuals as a group within any hospital—are still mostly not salaried employees of hospitals, creating the kinds of collaborative cultures in which all those working within a single patient care organization feel the same investment in the strategic and financial success of that organization, remains a challenge in the present.

This, interestingly, brings us back to the topic of performance improvement methodologies. One of the things that all those interviewed for this book agree on is that performance improvement methodologies are valuable to hospital performance improvement not only intrinsically—that is, because of the kinds of conceptual strategies they can bring to the leaders of quality and patient safety transformation—but also because of their objective, data-driven quality, and their language of equality and democracy. In other words, using performance improvement methodologies can not only speak to the core values of data-based objectivity and science to which physicians naturally adhere; but using these methodologies can also help overcome a lot of the terrible accretion of guild-based resentments, resistance, and anti-cohesion that have been a part of hospital organizations' corporate cultures for many decades. When multidisciplinary teams of clinicians sit down to review data-based studies and examine ways to improve clinical processes, they can shed the hats they wear in their disciplines day in and day out—primary care physician, specialist physician, nurse manager, floor nurse, respiratory therapist, pharmacist, phlebotomist, etc.—and become members of a synergistic team.

USE OF METHODOLOGIES SEEN AS HIGH POSITIVE

Certainly, those hospital leaders interviewed for this book express very strong satisfaction with their use of performance improvement methodologies. Asked whether the kinds of transformation taking place at the 44-hospital Trinity Health system could be achieved without the use of performance improvement methodologies (see pp. 86–95 for the Trinity Health system case study), Tammy Merkel, director of process excellence, says, flatly, "No. You need to apply some sort of process improvement methodology, whatever type you use," in order to obtain and sustain performance improvement results. "You have to have a plan. You have to execute it and act on it and check it out. And whether you're into Plan, Do, Check, Act, or Lean, or Six Sigma, you need a structure under which you can apply your activities. Otherwise, it just becomes too subjective, with people working without measurements, without a baseline, without a target."

What's more, says Merkel, "Part of any process improvement methodology is the whole concept of scoping and defining projects. Historically, many people not using a methodology skip that process," she notes. But she quickly adds, "You need to know what you're going to accomplish with a big process—not doing so means that you're opting to roam until you've figured it out, and ending up wasting time and resources."

In addition, says Merkel, "from a systems perspective, you often have very wide variation across an organization. And the first challenge is figuring out what critical items you can fix that will impact most strongly the entire organization." With 44 hospitals, all with their own processes and cultures, process improvement can become a Rubik's cube without the strategic use of methodologies to apply some standardization of work process and perspective. There is also the fact, says Merkel's colleague Laura Archbold, RN, a process improvement specialist-black belt at Trinity Health, "You can also have multiple process improvement efforts going on in the same hospital, yet they are unsynchronized. If we can achieve synergy, so that those efforts are working together, we can see greater improvement." Applying formal performance improvement methodologies, she says, is one element in creating that kind of synergy.

At Children's Hospital of Wisconsin, in Milwaukee (see pp. 57–62 for the full case study), Ramesh Sachdeva, MD, PhD, DBA, vice-president for quality and outcomes, notes that he and his colleagues "have very strong data" available to help them in their process improvement work; "we have a full department collecting and analyzing data. But we've also tried to take it a notch higher, which means we've affirmatively tried to bring many of the elements of the scientific approach to our work here, to match the methodology to the improvement challenge. Unlike many hospitals ... We do Six Sigma, Lean management, and PDSA/PDCA, all three running concurrently." Rather than cling to methodology orthodoxy, "We check to see which methodology fits each problem," he says.

The attitude of Sachdeva and his colleagues at Children's Hospital of Wisconsin is quickly emerging as a dominant one—that is, an approach of heterodoxy rather than orthodoxy, or applying the right methodology to the situation at hand. There are some organizations that are taking a strict approach and using only one major methodology, but they are among a small, and dwindling, minority, particularly as the use of the various methodologies expands across health care.

Finally, transformative quality leaders at some organizations also cite the boost to the overall energy level around the work of transformation that performance improvement methodologies can help supply.

"The biggest challenge we know with quality improvement is sustaining change. That's what process improvement has done for us," says Cynthia Barnard, director, quality strategies, at the 897-bed Northwestern Memorial Hospital, a prestigious academic medical center located in downtown Chicago. "We've created all-new resources in order to fully pursue process improvement here," notes Barnard—and the resources, including robust funding for performance improvement, have partly gone to the training of clinicians and others in formal methodologies at Northwestern Memorial, as they have at organizations like Trinity Health and others. For Barnard and her colleagues, it is not only the application of resources to the overall work of transformation that brings added value, but also, she says, the fact that using such methodologies can help to gather clinician and staff energies around the nitty-gritty work at hand in any hospital organization.

MAJOR PERFORMANCE IMPROVEMENT METHODOLOGIES

What are the main methodologies that patient care organizations are using? Among the most popular are Lean management and Six Sigma, with the actual Toyota Production System and PDCA (Plan-Do-Check-Act)/Balanced Scorecard also being increasingly used in health care.

Below are some explanations of the various methodologies being used.

Lean Management

The Lean management movement is so popular across a range of industries that it has its own institute, the Lean Enterprise Institute.

In their 1996 book *Lean Thinking,* James P. Womack and Daniel T. Jones define a set of five basic principles that characterize a lean enterprise.[2] According to Womack and Jones, Lean organizations:

- Specify value from the standpoint of the end customer by product family.
- Identify all the steps in the value stream for each product family, eliminating every step and every action and every practice that does not create value.
- Make the remaining value-creating steps occur in a tight and integrated sequence so the product will flow smoothly toward the customer.
- Let customers pull value from the next upstream activity as flow is introduced;
- Enable managers and teams to elimination further waste and pursue perfection through continuous improvement as these steps lead to greater transparency.

In other words, eliminating waste in production processes and redirecting human effort toward value-added activities are key elements. As the Lean Management Institute's Web site notes, Lean principles go back to Kiichiro Toyoda's founding of the Toyota Production System in the auto industry. The Web site notes that

> As Kiichiro Toyoda, Taiichi Ohno, and others at Toyota looked at this situation [of time, gas, and other auto production problems] in the 1930s, and more intensely just after World War II, it occurred to them that a series of simple innovations might make it more possible to provide both continuity in process flow and a wide variety in product offerings. They therefore revisited [Henry] Ford's original thinking, and invented the Toyota Production System. This system in essence shifted the focus on the manufacturing engineer from individual machines and their utilization, to the flow of the product through the total process.[3]

Therefore, the concept of flow was built into the idea of optimized production, and formed the basis for Lean management principles.

In health care, patient care organizations have used Lean principles to approach and attack many systemic problems, among the most important of which include streamlining core patient care delivery processes; optimizing clinician workflow; taking apart very complex clinical processes like medication management, analyzing them, and reengineering them; and finding ways to uncover systemic process causes of medical errors.

A variety of organizations have sprung up recently to spread Lean principles in health care. One of them, the Cork, Ireland-based Lean Healthcare Services, explains on its Web site that,

The essence of Lean Thinking as applied to health care is to:

- Eliminate waste through understanding the value to the patient and how to deliver that value.
- Create an efficient and waste-free continuous flow system built on a pull vs. 'batch and queue' approach.
- Continually pursue a perfect system. [4]

The organization's Web site goes on to add,

The following are examples of the types of wastes that exist in health care:

- Redundant capture of information on admission
- Multiple recording of patient information
- Excess supplies stored in multiple locations
- Time spent looking for charts
- Patient waiting rooms
- Continuous back-tracking of movement of medical staff
- Time spent waiting for equipment, lab results, x-rays, etc.
- Time spent dealing with complaints about service

Toyota Production System

Though Lean management principles are spreading across numerous industries and have begun to be applied in more and more patient care organizations, those principles have their clear origin in the Toyota Production System created for the manufacture of Toyota automobiles. Although Lean management principles are being studied and taught separately from the Toyota Production System (TPS), the two remain closely linked, both conceptually and in practice. Thus, books, articles, speakers, and seminars often deal with both.

For example, *Becoming Lean: Inside Stories of U.S. Manufacturers,* edited by Jeffrey K. Liker, PhD, deals with both.[5]

In Chapter 2 of the book, "Bringing the Toyota Production System to the United States: A Personal Perspective," author John Y. Shook outlines a number of core principles of TPS. These include:

- *Jidoka:* The Japanese word means "building in quality and designing operations and equipment so that people are not tied to machines but are free to perform value-added work that is appropriate for humans"
- Just-in-time: "the right part at the right time in the right amount"
- "One-piece flow" for maximum efficiency
- "Takt time," a concept whose use helps create just-in-time production

Of course, translating these concepts into health care takes some thought and work. But the general concepts such as streamlining workflow processes and creating value through individual work contributions are being applied in a variety of health care settings. At Virginia Mason Medical Center, as has been discussed earlier, a great deal of work has been focused on eliminating both waste in the production of patient care delivery, and eliminating medical errors.

Six Sigma

Another set of principles and practices that is moving into the health care industry but that originated in manufacturing is Six Sigma. As the online encyclopedia *Wikipedia* explains it:

> Six Sigma is a set of practices originally developed by Motorola to systematically improve processes by eliminating defects. . . . While the particulars of the methodology were originally formulated by Bill Smith at Motorola in 1986, Six Sigma was heavily inspired by six preceding decades of quality improvement methodologies such as quality control, TQM, and Zero Defects. Like its predecessors, Six Sigma asserts the following:

- Continuous efforts to reduce variation in process outputs is key to business success
- Manufacturing and business processes can be measured, analyzed, improved and controlled
- Succeeding at achieving sustained quality improvement requires commitment from the entire organization, particularly from top-level management[6]

Wikipedia goes on to note that the term "six sigma" refers to processes that operate with produce products at defect levels below 3.4 defects per one million opportunities. Six Sigma is a registered service mark and trademark of Motorola, Inc.

In health care, Six Sigma is being used to attack a variety of problems, from time efficiency-related ones to clinical care quality ones. In an online article entitled "Measuring Six Sigma Results in the Healthcare Industry," author Carolyn Pexton notes that,

The following represent some of the successful projects and initiatives taking place at hospitals and health systems throughout the United States, applying a combination of Six Sigma, Lean and change management methods:

- Projects at Thibodaux Regional Medical Center in Louisiana have yielded more than $4 million in revenue growth, cash flow improvement and cost savings.
- Good Samaritan Hospital in Los Angeles reduced registry expenses by mapping multiple process drivers and achieved cost savings between $5.5 and $6 million.
- Virtua Health in New Jersey has had a vigorous Six Sigma program in place for several years as part of their Star Initiative to achieve operational excellence. In one project focused on congestive heart failure, length of stay was reduced from 6 to 4 days; patient education improved from 27 to 80%; and chart consistency improved from 67 to 93%.
- Valley Baptist Health System in Harlingen, Texas, reduced surgical cycle time, adding capacity for an additional 1,100 cases per year and increasing potential revenue more than $1.3 million annually.
- Boston Medical Center improved throughput in diagnostic imaging, with a potential impact of more than $2.2 million in cost savings and revenue growth.

- The Women and Infants Hospital of Rhode Island successfully used Six Sigma and change management to standardize operating procedures for embryo transfer, yielding a 35% increase in implantation rates.[7]

As Pexton notes, health care organizations are generally mixing and combining a variety of approaches to process improvement in order to achieve the best results; few are using solely Six Sigma, Lean management, or the Toyota Production System.

Plan-Do-Check-Act/Balanced Scorecard

One additional methodology that some health care organizations are using is called "Plan-Do-Check-Act" (sometimes also referred to as "Plan-Do-Study-Act," as at Children's Hospital of Wisconsin), which has also been incorporated as a concept in Six Sigma. As *Wikipedia* explains it:

> PDCA was made popular by Dr. W. Edwards Deming, who is considered by many to be the father of modern quality control; however it was always referred to by him as the 'Shewhart cycle.' Later in Deming's career, he modified PDCA to 'Plan, Do, Study, Act' (PDSA) so as to better describe his recommendations. . . . In Six Sigma programs, this cycle is called 'Define, Measure, Analyze, Improve, Control' (DMAIC). . . . PDCA should be repeatedly implemented, as quickly as possible, in upward spirals that converge on the ultimate goal, each cycle closer than the previous. . . . This approach is based on the understanding that our knowledge and skills area always limited, but improving as we go. Often, key information is unknown, or unknowable. . . . Rather than enter 'analysis paralysis' to get it perfect the first time, it is better to be approximately right than exactly wrong. Over time and with better knowledge and skills, PDCA will help define the ideal goal, as well as help get us there.[8]

In health care, PDCA principles have been used in numerous instances in the context of the Balanced Scorecard (BSC) approach, which analyzes mission and strategy into objectives organized according to financial, customer, internal business process, and learning and growth perspectives.

In a 2003 article in *Managed Care Magazine*, Judith A. Shutt of Southwest Texas State University-San Marcos describes the use of PDCA within a Balanced Scorecard initiative pursued by Duke Children's Hospital.[9] Shutt writes that:

In the *Harvard Business Review,* the chief medical director at Duke Children's Hospital (DCH) in Durham, N.C., described one of the first successful implementations of the BSC in a large health care facility. In 1997, the average length of stay at DCH was eight days, or 20% longer than the national average. The average per-patient cost at DCH was $15,000 (more money than was being reimbursed); consequently, the hospital was faced with a projected $7 million increase in annual losses within four years. It was apparent that drastic measures had to be initiated quickly to preserve financial stability. The BSC was identified as the one management strategy that linked the four areas—finance, customer satisfaction, business processes, and staff satisfaction—and appeared to be the answer regarding both short- and long-term improvements.

After defining the organization's management requirements for meeting goals, the medical director began the implementation of the BSC in the pediatric intensive care unit (PICU). Within six months, the PICU reduced the cost per case by 12% and increased patient satisfaction by 8%. Reorganization, new protocols, and an emphasis on 'multidisciplinary teams focused on a particular illness or disease' were credited for the improvements (Meliones 2000). By 2000, the BSC was evidenced throughout DCH, and the hospital successfully lowered its cost per case by $5,000, leading to a net gain of $4 million.

A FEW WORDS OF CAUTION AND ADVICE

Experts in the various performance improvement methodologies may disagree on many things, but in one area, they tend to agree. For business organizations in any industry to successfully apply such methodologies, they need to do so strategically, and to create new cultures and ways of thinking, rather than to approach the available methodologies simply as tool kits whose individual tools can be used to "fix" small, discrete problems.

As Jeffrey Liker, PhD, author of *The Toyota Way: 14 Management Principles from the World's Greatest Manufacturer,* puts it,

> One of the things I was trying to accomplish with *The Toyota Way* was to counterbalance the concept of the idea of Lean as a toolkit. I think that whole way of thinking that there is something you can just pick up as a set

of tools to 'Lean out' a system, is a misunderstanding of the Toyota process. The reality is that Lean was an abstraction from observing Toyota, and that abstraction has been converted into a lot of different variations and flavors, which are being deployed en masse to many, many different kinds of businesses, and these things are very variable.[10]

Asked how health care organizations and other organizations outside auto manufacturing can apply Lean management principles successfully, Liker says that "The most important thing is that leadership from the top be both consistent and patient over the long term. If the leaders are consistent and patient, they will have success. And whether they use Kaizen workshops, value-stream mapping, or pilot projects," they will find success over time, if the leadership is right. Certainly, Liker says, the unusual incentive misalignments in health care, particularly the fact that physicians work in hospitals and other patient care organizations but are not their employees—pose special problems in health care, but the key is long-term leadership and a holistic approach to change.

In other words, a long-term cultural embrace of process change.

That sentiment is echoed by Gary Convis, who recently retired as president of Toyota Motor Manufacturing Kentucky, Inc. "My honest opinion," says Convis, who spent more than two decades at Toyota, "is that culture is so much more important than people realize. Most people don't even put it on the road map or recognize it as a critical component of how to actually get better. But I've been with Toyota 24 years, and in my first two weeks in Japan in 1984, I could feel a sense that I was encountering a culture that was not like anything I'd ever experienced before. And the reality is that if you're going to make any kind of change to an organization, culture is a substantial foundation issue."

The good news for health care executives, Convis says, is that TPS concepts are very flexible, and "totally, totally translatable. TPS," he says, "is about thinking and philosophy, and there are many, many ways to apply those philosophies to different subjects. And these things should become apparent when studying Toyota."

In fact, Convis says, the complex details of patient care processes share some similarities to some auto manufacturing processes:

Let's take the example of arc-welding. There may be some similarities here to the example of averting ventilator-acquired pneumonia through attention to the patient's bed position, that type of detail. In arc-welding, you have to achieve good mating service fitting when welding, so the joint between two pieces is quite close. The welding tip has to be at a certain angle and position and distance away from the metal; it has to be moving at a certain rate of speed; and the flow of the copper has to be at that speed; and the temperature settings of the welding have to be right.

Also, appropriately transferring the precise knowledge about how to handle that particular situation is in some ways analogous to clinicians sharing in an organized way information about bed position for the prevention of ventilator-acquired pneumonia.

In the end, Convis says, "It usually comes back to consistency of leadership, and priorities. We've been blessed with a leadership at Toyota that has had a certain philosophy and lived it."

NOTES

1. As cited in the article "Transforming Healthcare Organizations," Brian Golden, *Healthcare Quarterly*, 10(Sp) 2006:10–19. (accessed July 2008) http://www.long-woods.com/product.php?productid=18490.
2. Daniel T. Jones and James P. Womack, *Lean Thinking*. 1996, 2003, New York, Simon & Shuster. (accessed July 2008)
3. "Principles of Lean": http://www.lean.org/WhatsLean/Principles.cfm.
4. "Introducing Lean Healthcare": web description. Lean Healthcare Services website: http://www.leanhealthcareservices.com/leanexplained02.htm. (accessed July 2008)
5. Jeffrey K. Liker, ed. *Becoming Lean: Inside Stories of U.S. Manufacturers* (New York: Productivity Press, 1998).
6. *Wikipedia*, s.v. "Six Sigma," http://en.wikipedia.org/wiki/Six_Sigma.
7. http://healthcare.isixsigma.com/library/content/c040623a.asp.
8. *Wikipedia*, s.v. "Plan-Do-Check-Act, " http://en.wikipedia.org/wiki/PDCA.
9. "Balancing the Health Care Scorecard," Judith A. Shutt, Managed Care, September 2003, pp. 42–46. www.managedcaremag.com/archives/0309/0309.peer_balanced.pdf. (accessed July 2008)
10. Jeffrey K. Liker, *The Toyota Way: 14 Management Principles from the World's Greatest Manufacturer,* (New York: The McGraw-Hill Companies, 1994).

10

Policy Considerations and the Future of Transformative Quality

What should be clear to readers from the preceding chapters contexting the quality revolution, and describing the groundbreaking quality and patient safety work taking place among pioneer hospital organizations, is this: The quality revolution and its underlying quality imperative, are here to stay. Simply by sheer dint of the determination on the part of the leaders in pioneer organizations to push their organizations forward, work will continue and progress at the organizational level. Meanwhile, pay-for-performance programs such as the CMS/Premier HQID project are demonstrating that quality transformation can be encouraged at a national level, and achieve results beyond the individual organizational level and over time.

Still, the kinds of care quality and patient safety improvements being made by individual pioneer organizations are just that—individual organizations' leaps into the quality void, often involving heroic efforts and sustained commitments by organizational leaders willing to invest in quality and patient safety without any direct financial reward, except from the potential differential reimbursement coming from purchasers and payers in their individual markets that have established programs to reward highest-quality providers, or from participation in pay-for-performance programs such as the CMS/Premier HQID project.

What needs to happen on the reimbursement level is for the federal Medicare program, and for private insurers and state Medicaid programs as well, to use the levers of reimbursement to promote and reward innovation. At present, apart from the rewards coming out of the CMS/Premier P4P program and a few others, there is simply no financial incentive to pursue transformative quality work, while there are many disincentives, including the cost, and the underlying "negative" problem, the absence of rewards built into the system to actively promote adherence to the highest standards of quality and safety. Put very starkly, if everyone gets paid the same for a hospital stay with the same menu of services delivered, regardless of the level of quality, or even whether in some cases, some of those stays were prolonged by medical errors or other problems caused by some of the hospitals, what incentive is there for health care system-wide improvement? And how do executives and clinician executives convince the front-line caregivers and staff in most organizations to move forward in the absence of a broader "burning platform" for change, other than to invoke potential future consequences?

One area that has been somewhat beyond the scope of this book, but which should appropriately be included in any discussion of reimbursement reform, is that of disease management/chronic care management/ management of patients across the spectrum of care. Though it deserves its own coverage and analysis, I mention it here because it naturally fits into the broader category of rewarding outcomes more generally, rather than being procedure-based. Combining reimbursement for care partly based on the measured quality and patient safety of that care, with care management that went beyond single episodes of inpatient care, would mean rewarding clinicians and patient care organizations for seeing to the broader needs of patients, and averting re-hospitalizations, appropriately shortening lengths of stay (as they prevented the medical errors and gaps in care that now add to those lengths).

Were the health care system—at the federal level, through Medicare, as well as at the state level via Medicaid programs, and among all major private health insurers, with the help and encouragement of private purchasers—to move towards such a new model, the transformation of care quality and patient safety across the U.S. health care system could be accelerated phenomenally. Absent significant reimbursement changes, quality transformation will remain the province of those hospital-based organizations (and some larger medical groups) willing to forge ahead for the sake of quality itself. If policymakers in Washington and in the state capitals want more, they need to reform our payment systems to encourage innovation and fundamental change in the health care delivery system.

Thus, I would propose three key policy innovations, and I will explain them in sequence:

- First, that a federal fund be created to support an annual nationwide competition similar to that of the Malcolm Baldrige Award, but specifically pertaining to care quality and patient safety improvement, with very detailed criteria and specific categories for achievement in those areas, for hospitals and integrated health systems (and with an adjunct award for physician groups), with a significant purse for prizes and discrete funding for the use of that competition to amass a data warehouse/catalog of best practices and to produce white papers and other documents arising out of the competition's activity, to further stimulate improvement nationwide.

- Second, that federal reimbursement incentives be created for the following:
  - Funding set aside in the form of individual grants for hospitals and health systems to create quality offices within their organizations to lead and stimulate quality work (following the model of the Center for Clinical Excellence at Brigham and Women's Hospital in Boston (see case study, pp. 44–53).
  - The explicit reformulation of both Medicare and Medicaid reimbursement in order to reward chronic disease management care and coordinated care across the spectrum of patient care, including the concept of the "medical home."
  - The explicit reformulation of both Medicare and Medicaid reimbursement in order to expand pay-for-payment programs across the Medicare program generally.
  - Explicit reimbursement support for clinical IT implementation to improve clinical care quality and patient safety (support for hospital-based organizations and medical groups alike).
- As a corollary to the establishment of those federal reimbursement incentives, private health insurers and state Medicaid programs should follow the Medicare program's lead as that program introduces the above payment innovations, and reinforce the same kinds of performance innovations and the implementation of facilitative clinical information systems.
- Third, that a non-punitive nationwide database and online publishing organization be set up at a federal level. That organization need not be in the form of a federal agency; rather, some version of a research foundation model could be quite workable. That organization's sole purpose would be nationwide data development, to provide best practices data and information across the spectrum of quality and patient safety learnings industry-wide.

Per the preceding proposals, to begin with, it seems clear from what has occurred with regard to the Baldrige Award that the health care system can be stimulated by a combination of incentives. In the first proposal, the amount of money dedicated annually to an award program would not need to be enormous; nor would it all need to come from federal coffers. Progressive employers and broad business alliances should logically support such a program. What's more, by creating a permanent awards program with a data collection and data-sharing component regarding best practices, such a program could invite very broad nationwide participation.

The second set of proposals are somewhat self-explanatory; but the idea would be to reward intensive, organization-wide quality and patient safety improvement work; to reward bundled/coordinated care; to expand the pay-for-performance concept, as initiated in the CMS/Premier HQID demonstration project; and to explicitly support clinical IT implementation to further care quality and patient safety work. In all of these instances, the lack of funding to stimulate such work is hindering its advancement.

In the third proposal, creating a nationwide database to share data and best practices could provide a true data foundation for hospital, medical group, and health system data-sharing at a nationwide level. That proposal could be combined with the awards program proposal, and could support it.

At the same time, it is also inevitable that some of the elements of what's being called "non-pay for non-performance" will advance at the federal level and among private insurers, such as the Medicare's recently initiated "never events" list of procedures the program will no longer pay for. Though I do not specifically advocate non-payment for non-performance, I believe it will end up becoming an inevitable "other side of the coin" of the pay-for-performance programs that are one element in the skein of new incentives that can help move the health care system forward.

The millions of dollars paid out by CMS in the CMS/Premier HQID project, and the across-the-board improvements in care quality and patient safety among participating HQID hospitals, demonstrate that payment incents change. What's more, the creation in the past year of Premier's new QUEST program, which is zeroing in even more closely on the attempt to improve patient safety and quality in the nation's hospitals while safely reducing costs, adds to the evidence that incenting change can be successful with regard to all types of hospital organizations. Over time, physician organizations will be brought even more fully into pay for performance as well, as they have been by the massive California P4P demonstration project.

PEERING INTO THE FUTURE

The previous discussion of potential policy and reimbursement changes underscores the very long journey ahead towards quality transformation facing the U.S. health care system. As policymakers and industry observers agree, our system may be out of the starting gates when it comes to a journey of the archetypal 1,000 miles; but we're still in a very, very early phase. There are so many aspects of care quality and patient safety improvement that are only beginning to be explored; and the number of pioneer organizations in this area remains extremely small as a percentage of all hospital-based organizations in the United States. Yet the fact of successes to date on the part of some of those pioneers shows that progress is possible; while the demands for improvement, and for the documentation of improvement, coming from public and private purchasers and payers, indicate that the pressures towards improvement, and towards transparency, will only intensify and accelerate over time. The combination of cost pressures, demographic changes, growing purchaser (and ultimately, consumer) activism on value, and the expanding catalog of early successes on the part of pioneer organizations, all speak to the underlying wave of change that is pushing patient care organizations forward.

In this necessary journey, one can only hope for the best kinds of change, and try to contribute in some individual way towards the accomplishment of that change. This author's most fervent hope is that twenty years from now, we will all look back on this time in satisfaction over the massive forward-moving changes that will have been made in the intervening time, and wonder why quality transformation was ever an issue in the U.S. health care system to begin with.

As mentioned in Chapter 1, the quote from the Roman orator Seneca, though uttered 2,000 years ago and in a very different context, is one that couldn't be more appropriate to the current situation. As the health care system moves forward on quality and patient safety, Seneca's words should echo in the minds of health care executives, clinicians, and staff nationwide: "The gods guide those willing to change; those unwilling, they drag."

About the Author

Mark Hagland is a national award-winning health care journalist, author, and speaker with nearly 20 years' experience covering a diverse array of industry issues, from health care policy to quality and patient safety, to provider-payer relations, strategic planning, governance, and information technology subjects. His first book, *Paradox and Imperatives: How Efficiency, Effectiveness, and E-Transformation Can Conquer Waste and Optimize Quality,* co-authored with noted health care economist and futurist Jeffrey C. Bauer, PhD, was published by Productivity Press in January 2008.

A former executive editor of *Hospitals & Health Networks* magazine, Hagland has been an independent health care journalist since 1996. In 1997, he was the national winner in the trade publication category of the National Institute for Health Care Management's Fourth Annual Health Care Journalism Award, for a cover story he wrote for *California Medicine* on the challenges of the IPA (Independent Practice Association) model of physician governance. His three-part cover story series on patient safety issues for *Healthcare Informatics* received a bronze regional award from the American Society of Business Publication Editors in 2006. In addition the article he and Jeffrey Bauer co-wrote for *Healthcare Financial Management* on the emergence of consumer-directed health care won the Helen Yeger/L. Vann Seawell Best Article Award for 2006/2007 from the Healthcare Financial Management Association. Hagland continues to write for a wide variety of professional publications in health care and to speak to a range of executive and governance audiences. He has a BA in English from the University of Wisconsin and a master's degree in journalism from the Medill School of Journalism at Northwestern University. He lives in Chicago, Illinois.

Index

A

Abecassis, Michael, 83–84
Accreditation Council for Graduate
    Medical Education, recommen-
    dations by, 47
Acute myocardial infarction, 21
ADE alert system, 93
Adverse drug events, 4–6, 21, 34, 44,
    53–57, 76, 107–110, 124, 132. *See
    also* Barcoding medications;
    Radio-frequency medication
    identification
Agency for Healthcare Research and
    Quality, 18, 20–22, 81
AHRQ. *See* Agency for Healthcare
    Research and Quality
Air embolisms, 16
American Society of Health-System
    Pharmacists, Best Practices
    Award, 112
AMI. *See* Acute myocardial infarction
Anderson, Jay, 86
Archbold, Laura, 88–89, 92–95, 142
Australia, health care expenditures, 2
Austria, annual health care expenditures,
    2
Authority, informal, dealing with, 57
Auto manufacturing processes, patient
    care processes, similarities to,
    10, 150
Automation, use in health care, 36, 64,
    94–95, 106, 118, 121, 127–128,
    xviii

B

Balanced Scorecard, data analysis, 52, 148
Baldrige Award, 154
Bankowitz, Richard, 25–26
Barcoding medications, 128, 154
Barnard, Cynthia, 77–78, 80, 141, 143
Batalden, Paul B., 12–13
Bauer, Jeffrey C., 5, 159
*Becoming Lean: Inside Stories of U.S.
    Manufacturers,* 146
Bed sores, 33

Berkowitz, Lyle, 135–136
Bertolini, Mark, 33
Berwick, Donald, 27, 103
Best Practices Award, American Society of
    Health-System Pharmacists, 112
Beta blockers, 21, 103
Betty Irene Moore Nursing Initiative, 56
Bland, Mary, 104
Blood clots, hospital-acquired, 33
Blood donation identification system, 83
Blood incompatibility, 15–16, 31
Blood infections, hospital-acquired, 31
Blood poisoning, 33
Blood product identification, verification,
    61–62
Blue Cross and Blue Shield Association, 16
Board support, lack of, 31
Bond, C. A., 56
Boston Medical Center, 147
Brigham and Women's Hospital, 7–8,
    45–46, 124, 155
"Bringing Toyota Production System
    to United States: A Personal
    Perspective," 146
Broad vision, lack of, 31
BSC. *See* Balanced Scorecard
Buffalo General Hospital, 101
Buffington, Kimberly, overdosing twins
    of, Cedars-Sinai Medical Center,
    3, 32

C

Cabansag, R.N., 79
CABG. *See* Coronary artery bypass graft
California, rural areas in, Web-based
    health care technology, 98–100
California Health Care Foundation, 24
California Nursing Outcomes Coalition,
    57–58
CalNOC. *See* California Nursing
    Outcomes Coalition
Canada, health care expenditures, 2
Cardamone, Stephen, 113
Cardiac surgery patients, glucose levels in,
    114–117

Care Transformation Team, development of, 91
Casale, Alfred, 41, 67–68, 72
Cassano, Angela T., 79, 86
Catheter-associated infections, 16
Cedars-Sinai Medical Center, 3, 32, 126
Center for Clinical Excellence, 7–8, 46–56, 155
Center for Health Professions, San Francisco, 56
Center for Leadership and Improvement, 12
Center for Studying Health System Change, 10, 12
Centers for Medicare and Medicaid Services, 16–18, 25–28, 38–39, 41, 153–154, 156
CEO, perspective of, 41–42, 71–72
Cerner Corporation, 74
Charitable organizations, early hospitals sponsored as, xiv
CHCF. *See* California Health Care Foundation
Chest infections, after coronary artery bypass graft, 15–16
Children's Hospital of Wisconsin, 45, 60–64, 124, 130–131, 142–143, 148
CHW. *See* Children's Hospital of Wisconsin
Clancy, Carolyn, 12, 22
Clinical Pharmacy Program, emergency department, medication error reduction, 109–111
CMS. *See* Centers for Medicare and Medicaid Services
Commonwealth Fund, 27, 43
Complexity of health care system, 1
Computerized physician order entry, 63, 93, 123
Confusion over organization goals, 1
Consensus regarding elements in achieving physicians buy-in, 117
Contaminated devices, 34
Continuous quality improvement, 31
shortcomings of, xix
Contradictions in health care system, 2
Contradictory incentives, 2
Convis, Gary, 150
Core principles, 68–69
Coronary artery bypass graft, 41, 66
chest infections after, 15–16

CQI. *See* Continuous quality improvement
Criticism, vulnerability of U.S. health care system to, 3
Crossing the Quality Chasm, 43, 103
CSC Corporation, 132–133
Custodialism in health care, reversing tradition of, 37–38

D

Dartmouth-Hitchcock Leadership Preventive Medicine Residency, 12
Dartmouth-Hitchcock Medical Center, 12
Davis, Michael W., 127–130, 137
dbMotion, 74–76, xi
Decatur Memorial Hospital, 125
Define, Measure, Analyze, Improve, Control cycle, 146. *See also* Six Sigma
Definition of transformative quality, 31–44
Delivery, shoulder dystocia, care optimization, 84–85
Deming, W. Edwards, 148
Department of Health and Human Services, 12
Agency for Healthcare Research and Quality, 18
"Development, Testing, and Findings of a Pediatric-Focused Trigger Tool to Identify Medication-Related Harm in U.S. Children's Hospitals," 4
Diabetic patients, 20–21
hospital admissions, 21
Diamond, Joel, 76
Dilation, heart attack patients with occluded vessel, 101–102
Door-to-dilation, for heart attack patients, 9, 103–104, 107
Draper, Debra, 12, 14
Drazen, Erica, 132–133
Drucker, Peter, 1–2, 37, 139
Drug events, adverse, 4–5, 21, 34, 55–57, 78, 109–111, 125. *See also* Barcoding medications; Radio-frequency medication identification
Drug plan payments, 18
Duke Children's Hospital, 148–149

Dystocia, shoulder, care optimization, 84–85

E

Early involvement for physicians, need for, 116
EHRs. *See* Electronic health records
Eighty-hour rule, imposition of, 47
EKG, timely administration of procedure, 103–104
Electronic health records, 8, 36, 88, 93, 118, xviii
Electronic Medical Record Adoption Model, 127–130
Electronic medical records, 36, 74, 92–94, 123, 134, xviii
eMAR, implementation of, 132
Emergency department, clinical pharmacy program, medication errors reduction, 109–111
Emergency department model, University of Rochester Medical Center, 112
Emergency department trauma center, 61
Employer-sponsored plans, Medicare payments, 18
Empowerment of nurses, 57–59
EMR. *See* Electronic medical record
EMRAM. *See* Electronic Medical Record Adoption Model
Energy level, increase, with performance improvement methodologies, 143
Enterprise-wide clinical information sharing, 130
Epic [outpatient information] system, Epic Systems Corporation, 74, 76
Errors averted through, 79
Ethnography, nurses' flow, work patterns, 58
Evidence-driven quality, 65–87
Executive WalkRounds, 53–54
Expenditures on health care, 2, 18

F

Facilitative role of information technology, 122–123
Fahey, Linda, 125
Fairbanks, Rollin J., 110–112
Fairview Northland Medical Center, 26

Falls in hospitals, 33
FDA. *See* Food and Drug Administration
Federal budget, 18
Fera, Bill, 65, 73–76
"Five rights" of medication administration, 57
Florida, rural areas in, Web-based health care technology, 98–101
Flow, work patterns of nurses, ethnography, 58
Flynn, Ellen, 61–63
Food and Drug Administration, adverse drug events reported to, 34
Foot examination, diabetic patients, 21
Ford, Henry, 144
Foreign objects left in patient's body post-surgery, 15–16
Fortin, Jason, 132
France, annual health care expenditures, 2
Fraudulent medical claims, xv
Frustration with quality of U.S. health care, 3
Fuhrmans, Vanessa, 32–33
Future of transformative quality, 153–157

G

Gandhi, Tejal, 46–49, 53–55
Garets, Dave, 127–128, 130
Geisinger Health System, 42–43, 66–73
Geisinger Heart Institute, 40–41
Geisinger Medical Center, 67
Geisinger Quality Institute, 71
Genesis project, 93–95, 124
Georgia, rural areas in, Web-based health care technology, 98–101
Germany, annual health care expenditures, 2
Glucose monitoring, 114–115
Good Samaritan Hospital, 147
Gordon and Betty Moore Foundation, 56
Gottlieb, Gary, 51
Grobman, William, 84–85
Gross domestic product, U.S., spent on health care, 32
Guaranteed-price-for-surgery program, 41
Gustafson, Michael, 8, 46–50, 51, 55

H

Hackensack University Medical Center, 25
Haug, Peter, 125

Hays, Daniel P., 110–112
Health care expenditures, 2, 17, 21–24, 30
Health records, electronic, 9, 34, 93–96,
    118–119, xvi
Healthcare Information and Management
    Systems Society, 127–132
    Leadership Survey, 130–131
Heart attack patients
    counseling to quit smoking, 19
    dilation, occluded vessel, 103–104
    door-to-dilation for, 103–104
Hematology/oncology/transplant unit,
    61–63
Hemoglobin A1c measurement, diabetic
    patients, 21
Hepatic coma and hepatitis C, 76
Herbal supplements, role in medication
    effectiveness, 81
Hess, David, 99–102
HIMSS. *See* Healthcare Information and
    Management Systems Society
Hip replacements, standardization of care,
    91–92
Hod HaSharon, dbMotion software firm,
    74
Home health care, Medicare payments, 18
Homer Warner Center for Informatics
    Research, 125
Hopkins, Leo Nelson, 101–102
Hospice care, Medicare payments, 18
Hospital-acquired infections. *See*
    Infections, hospital-acquired
Hospital contracts, stipulations regarding
    "never events," 34
Hospital Quality and Safety Survey, 24
Hospital Quality Incentive
    Demonstration, 25–27, 38–39,
    41, 118, 153, 156
Hospitality services, use of performance
    improvement methodologies, 10
Hostels, original hospitals as, 37
HSC. *See* Center for Studying Health
    System Change
HUMC. *See* Hackensack University
    Medical Center

I

IHI. *See* Institute for Healthcare
    Improvement
*Improving America's Hospitals: The Joint
    Commission's Annual Report on
    Quality and Safety 2007,* 35–36

Incompatible blood error, 33
Industrial Revolution, 36
Industry-wide challenge of practice pat-
    tern variation, 89–90
Inertia, organizational, challenge of, 31
Infections, hospital-acquired
    after coronary artery bypass graft,
        15–16
    blood infections, 33
    catheter-associated, 15–16, 33
    Surgical Site Infection Prevention
        project, 114
    surgical site infections, 33, 114
    urinary tract infections, 15–16, 33
Informal authority, dealing with, 59
Information Age Revolution, 36
Information technology, 97, 121–137
    facilitative role of, 122–124
    implementation stages, 127–129
    outpatient applications, 135–136
    poorly implemented, as hindrance to
        quality, 121–122
    priorities in, 130
    reimbursement support, 155
    relationship between transformative
        quality and, 156
Infusion pumps, 78–79
INLP. *See* Integrated Nurse Leadership
    Program
Institute for Healthcare Improvement,
    8–9, 13, 27–28, 37, 39, 114
    grantee program, 104–105
    hospital collaboration, 113
    Pursuing Perfection grants, 38
Institute for Safe Medication Practices, 34
Institute of Medicine, 5, 20, 43, 56, 71, xvi
"Insurers Stop Paying for Care Linked to
    Errors: Health Plans Say New
    Rules Improve Safety and Cut
    Costs; Hospitals Can't Dun
    Patients," 32–33
Integrated Nurse Leadership Program,
    54–57
Integrated Patient Safety Team, 49
Intermountain Healthcare, 125
IT. *See* Information technology

J

JCAHO. *See* Joint Commission on
    Accreditation of Healthcare
    Organizations
Jidoka, usage of term, 146

Joint Commission on Accreditation of
Healthcare Organizations, 16,
35–36, 46, 50, 53, 58
Jones, Daniel T., 144
Just-in time, usage of term, 146

K

Kaiser Family Foundation, 3, 18,
Kaiser Permanente-Fremont, 56
Kaiser Permanente-Hayward, 56
Kaleida Health, 100–101
Kliger, Julie, 56, 57–58
Kramer, J. Michael, 92, 94–95, 97

L

Lack of standardized process creation in
health care, reasons for, 140–141
Lateral-level management, dealing with,
59
Lean Enterprise Institute, 144
Lean Healthcare Services, 145
Lean Management performance improve-
ment methodology, 10, 36, 61,
63, 143–150
Lean Thinking, 144
Leapfrog Group, 23–24, 51–52
Lee, Peter, 23
Legs, blood clots in, hospital-acquired, 33
Liker, Jeffrey K., 146, 149–150
Limb, incorrect, operations on, 33
Linscott, Karen, 23–24
Litigation, threat of, xiv, xv
Low-income subsidy payments, Medicare
payments, 18
Lungs, blood clots in, hospital-acquired,
31

M

MacArthur, Barbara, 40, 102–106
MacArthur, Richard, 105,
Manufacturing processes, patient care
processes, similarities to,
150–151
Market and Policy Monitor Program, 24,
43
McClellan, Mark, 16
MCG. *See* Medical College of Georgia
McKinley, Karen, 71
"Measuring Six Sigma Results in the
Healthcare Industry," 147–148

Medicaid programs, 16–18, 25–28, 38–39,
118, 153–155
Medical College of Georgia, 87, 99–102
Medical malpractice litigation, threat of,
xiv, xv
Medical Record Institute, 134
Medical records, electronic, 36, 74, 93–96,
123, 134, xvi
Medical Records Institute, 134
Survey of Electronic Medical Records
Trends and Usage, 131
Medicare, 3, 13, 15–18, 21, 24, 26, 33–34,
38, 118, 153–156
annual expenditures, 16
Part A, 3, 18
Part B, 18
Part C, 18
payments by type of service, 18
reimbursement levels, 155–156
Medication administration, 57
errors in, 3–5, 18, 30, 32, 55–59, 76,
110–113, 126 (*See also* Barcoding
medications; Radio-frequency
medication identification)
"five rights" of, 57
Medication barcoding, 131
Medication reconciliation process, 81–82,
92
Medieval Europe, hospitals established
during, 37
Merkel, Tammy, 89–90, 96, 142
MetaStar, 114
Metzger, Jane, 132
Miller, J. Roscoe, 83
Misidentification errors, transplant
organs, 82–84
Moore, Thomas J., 34
Motorola, Inc., 146–147
Multidisciplinary rounding, 115–116
Multidisciplinary team, advances created
from, 50

N

National Committee for Quality Health
Care, 51
National Healthcare Quality Report,
19–21
National Patient Safety Goals, 35
National Quality Form, stipulations
regarding "never events" in
hospital contracts, 33–34
National Quality Health Care Award, 51

Natural leadership, turnover of, 107–108
Novato Community Hospital, 56
NCQHC. *See* National Committee for Quality Health Care
"Never events," stipulations regarding, in hospital contracts, 33–34
NHQR. *See* National Healthcare Quality Report
NMPG. *See* Northwestern Memorial Physicians Group
Northwestern Memorial Hospital, 65, 77–86, 123, 135–136, 143
Northwestern Memorial Physicians Group, 135–136
Norway, health care expenditures, 2
Noskin, Gary, Northwestern Memorial, 80–82

O

Office of Management and Budget, 3, 18
Office of Value Purchasing in Medicare, 23
Ohno, Taiichi, 144
One-piece flow, usage of term, 146
Operating on wrong limb, 33
Operative instruments, left in patient after surgery, 33–34
Organ transplant errors, 82–84
Organ transplant identification verification, 82–84
Organizational inertia, challenge of, 31
Orthopedic surgery patients, standardization of care, 91–92
Outpatient care, expanding information technology to, 135–136
Overcoming physician resistance to standardization, 105–106

P

Pacific Business Group on Health, 23
PACS. *See* Picture archiving and communications system
Paradox and Imperatives in Health Care: How Efficiency, Effectiveness, and E-Transformation Can Conquer Waste and Optimize Quality, 5–6, 66
Paradox in relationship between transformative quality, information technology, 121

Participation by physicians, as critical element in physician buy-in, 116–117
Partisan gridlock, prevention of governments solutions, 6
Partnership, clinical cultures of, 109–119
Patient-centric approaches, 113–119
Patient Safety Leadership WalkRounds, 7–8, 46–49
Patient Safety Team, 49–52, 53
Paulus, Ronald A., 69
Payson, Carol, 79–80
Pediatric intensive care unit, 61–64, 149
Penicillin-like drugs, recording in information system, 74
Performance Excellence initiative, 118
Performance improvement methodologies, 10, 139–151. *See also under* specific methodology
Pexton, Carolyn, 147–148
Picture archiving and communications system, xviii
PICU. *See* Pediatric intensive care unit
Pioneering organizations, common characteristics shared by, 9–11
Plan-Do-Check-Act performance improvement methodology, 10, 34–35, 61, 142–149
Pneumonia, from ventilator use, 35, 124
Point-of-care data collection, 128
Policy considerations, 153–157
Political infighting, challenges of, 31
Poorhouses, original hospitals as, 37
Poorly implemented information technology, as hindrance to quality transformation, 122–123
Post-operative patients, glucose levels in, 113–116
Premier, Inc., 25–27, 38–40, 43, 153, 156–157
Premier P4P program, 153
Pressure ulcers, 15–16
Private health expenditures, growth in, 17–18
Project Genesis, 94–95, 124
Prosecution, fraudulent medical claims, xv
ProvenCare program, 41–43, 65–72
Pursuing Perfection program, 8–9, 38, 87, 102–104, 107

Q

Quaid, Dennis, twins of, overdosing at Cedars-Sinai Medical Center, 3–5, 32
Quality Outcomes Group, 52
QUEST program, 156–157

R

Radio-frequency medication identification, 128
Rapid-response teams, 103–104
REACH Call Web-based technology, 99–101
Reinertsen, James, 37, 42–44
Reinertsen Group, 37
Religious denominations, early hospitals sponsored by, xiv
Retinal eye examination, diabetic patients, 21
RFID. *See* Radio-frequency medication identification
Rogness, Barbara, 114–117
Rural health care markets, Web-based technology, 98–102

S

Sachdeva, Ramesh, 45, 60–64, 142–143
San Francisco Bay area hospitals, 9, 45
San Francisco Bay Area hospitals, medication administration errors, 55–59
San Francisco Center for Health Professions, 56
San Francisco General Hospital, 56
Schade, Sue, 48, 52
Schoenbaum, Stephen C., 27, 43–44
Semantic interoperability, 74
Senior executives, 42
Sequoia Hospital, 56
Shannon, Maribeth, 24, 43
Shared Governance Council, 116
Shewhart cycle, 148
Shinn, Alyssa, dosage error, mortality from, 5
Shook, John Y., 146
Shoulder dystocia care, 84–85
Shutt, Judith A., 148
Six Sigma performance improvement methodology, 10, 36, 61–63, 124, 142–149

Skilled nursing facilities, Medicare payments, 18
"Smart" infusion pumps, 78–79
Smith, Bill, 146
Smoking-cessation counseling, 21
South Carolina, rural areas in, Web-based health care technology, 98–101
Specimens, mislabeled, 62–63
Spending on health care, 2, 17
St. Joseph Mercy Oakland, 95
St. Rose Hospital, 56
Stanford Hospital and Clinics, 56
Steele, Glenn Jr., 41, 67–69, 71–73
Stipulations regarding "never events," in hospital contracts, 34–35
Stroke, 87
    reading stroke scale, 101
    Stroke Team hotline, 105
    symptoms of, 98
    telemedicine-based care, 99–103
    Web-based technology, rural health care markets, 98–102
Suppliers, Medicare payments, 18
Sweden, health care expenditures, 2
Switzerland, annual health care expenditures, 2

T

Takata, Glenn S., 4
Takt time, usage of term, 146
Tallahassee Memorial Hospital, 8–9, 39–41, 87, 102–108
    reducing mortality rates, 87, 98–108
Teaching culture of quality, 70–71
Telemedicine-based acute stroke care program, Medical College of Georgia, 99–100
Tessier, Claudia, 134
Texas, rural areas in, Web-based health care technology, 98–101
Thibodaux Regional Medical Center, 147
Thomason Healthcare, 51
"Thomson Top 100 Hospitals," 51
Threat of medical malpractice litigation, xiv, xv
To Err Is Human, 5, 20, 103, xiv
Total knee replacements, standardization of care, 91–92
Total quality management, 31
    shortcomings of, xvii

Toyoda, Kiichiro, 144
Toyota Motor Manufacturing Kentucky, Ind., 150–151
Toyota Production System, 10, 36–37, 144–150
The Toyota Way: 14 Management Principles from the World's Greatest Manufacturer, 149–150
tPA, timely administration of, for stroke, 98
TPS. *See* Toyota Production System
TQM. *See* Total quality management
Traditional way of preparing infused medication, 78
Transparency, 66–70, 101–104, 117–119
Transplant identification verification, 82
Trinity Health, 8, 87–97, 124, 141–143
Turf battles, challenges of, 31
Turisco, Fran, 133
Turnover of natural leadership, 107–108

U

UHC. *See* University HealthSystem Consortium
Ulcers, pressure, 15–16
Union-sponsored plans, Medicare payments, 18
United Kingdom, health care expenditures, 2
University HealthSystem Consortium, 51
University of California, San Francisco's Center for Health Professions, 56
University of Pittsburgh Medical Center, 65, 73–76
University of Rochester Medical Center, 109–111
Unlabeled specimens, 59–60
UPMC. *See* University of Pittsburgh Medical Center
Urinary tract infections, catheter-associated, 15–16, 33

URMC. *See* University of Rochester Medical Center

V

Vaginal delivery, shoulder dystocia during, 84
Valley Baptist Health System, 147
Values within health care system, confusion over, 1
Vendors, integrating products from, 133
Ventilator use, pneumonia with, 124
Virginia Mason Medical Center, 146
Virtua Health, 147
Vitamins, interaction with medications, 81
Vulnerability of U.S. health care system to criticism, 3

W

WalkRounds, 7–8, 46–49, 52–53
Web-based health care technology, 98–102
Weems, Kerry, M.C., 17, 39
Weigle, Carl G. M., 63–64, 124, 131–132
WellPoint, Inc., 16, 33
Wheaton Franciscan Healthcare, 109, 113–118
Whittington, John, 124
Wisconsin Collaborative for Health Care Quality, 118
Womack, James P., 144
Wrong limb, operating on, 33

Y

Young patients, vulnerability to medical errors, 60

Z

Zero Defects quality improvement methodology, 146
Zoph, Tim, 123